JEDIDIAH MORSE

NUMBER TWO

COLUMBIA STUDIES IN
AMERICAN CULTURE

Jedidiah Morse

JEDIDIAH MORSE

A CHAMPION
OF NEW ENGLAND
ORTHODOXY

JAMES KING MORSE

NEW YORK : MORNINGSIDE HEIGHTS
COLUMBIA UNIVERSITY PRESS
1939

To
My Wife
M E D I A

PREFACE

"IF SOME future historian of the church shall relate, that in the beginning of the nineteenth century, in a country whose constitution secures the freedom of religious opinion, and requires only a general belief of the Christian religion, a set of men combined to write down all who ventured to think for themselves, to raise the cry of heresy against those who preferred the scriptures as the rule of their faith to any human creed, it certainly will be deemed incredible." John Lowell predicted in 1815 that "posterity will require some collateral evidence of the fact. They will search the records of our historical societies, and the alcoves of our colleges, for any controversial writings which may confirm so improbable a story."

The following essay is an attempt to reveal, by documentary evidence, the intricate religious pattern and the "incredible story" of a formative and confused period in our American church history—1783–1819—as it is reflected in the mind and career of that protagonist of orthodoxy, Jedidiah Morse. No attempt is here made to write a biography. Only his participation in the controversies of his day is described, the aim of this study being to clarify the general issues at stake.

This study has been made possible largely through the availability of many hitherto unpublished letters of Jedidiah Morse. For the use of this material, I am indebted to the Yale University Library and to the New York Public Library. A list of those unpublished letters which contain material directly pertinent to this study will be found on pages 194 and 195, together with page references to excerpts from these letters given in the text.

PREFACE

I am particularly grateful to Professor Herbert W. Schnei-
der for his stimulating criticism and patient encouragement,
and to Professor William Walker Rockwell for his valuable
suggestions and counsel.

CONTENTS

JEDIDIAH MORSE

CHAPTER I

INTRODUCTION

AFTER the emotional upheaval of the "Great Awakening" the churches of New England settled down to relative peace. A growing number of sober liberals felt more certain than ever that no permanent good for the cause of religion could come from this emotional appeal. At the same time many Old Calvinists complacently used the opportunity to reaffirm their fundamental beliefs as the only sound principles. Both these rationalists and Calvinists pointed to increasing dissension as the fruit of "the late period of enthusiasm," and made common cause against the group of New Lights who were carrying on the Awakening and developing the Edwardean convictions into what was expected to be a dwindling sect. But the calm was brief. The Old Calvinists and the New Lights, both sensed the threat to their common beliefs coming from a new enemy, Socinianism or Unitarianism. They were drawn together in the impending struggle, temporarily compromising their theological differences. This trend is illustrated in the successive careers of Presidents Clap, Stiles, and Dwight of Yale College, for in Timothy Dwight the new issues emerged clearly and in him the combined forces of Calvinism and Edwardeanism found their first vigorous champion against "infidelity."

President Clap began as an Old Calvinist. He had feared the disturbance resulting from the revivals of the "New Lights" and worked to prevent them. But when the same New Light brethren were attacked by the latitudinarian opposers, the president joined forces with the former.[1] "His theological opinions had not been modified but he sustained the policy adopted by the New Light party in the General Assembly, and on this account was called a political New Light." [2]

The successor to President Clap was Ezra Stiles—"a moderate Calvinist, if this appellation belongs to one who is sensible of difficulties connected with the doctrines of his system, as well as confident of the solid grounds on which these doctrines rest; who observes a certain modesty on the deep matters of Predestination and Original Sin, lest by an imperfect statement, or utterance of a half-truth, he should repel or confuse an honest mind." [3] Stiles went through a long period of doubt and study before he could reaffirm the Old Calvinism. "About 1747," he wrote, "till which time I was full of the sentiments of Calvinism, I had great solicitude about my being elected." [4] He was troubled because of his inability to give a rational interpretation to his religion. He yearned to have the same kind of proof for his theology as for natural science. He fought through his intellectual battle until he could claim that he had "reason to believe the doctrines of grace, exhibited in the confessions drawn up at the Reformation, and particularly held by the Puritan divines in England, and the venerable fathers of the New England churches." [5]

Having thus attained an Old Calvinist conviction by means of new reasons, Stiles seemed to be acceptable to the New Divinity group. According to a letter from Jonathan Edwards

[1] For a statement of the controversy between Old Lights and New Lights in Connecticut, see George C. Groce, Jr., "Benjamin Gale." (*New England Quarterly*, Vol. X, Number 4, 1937.)

[2] G. P. Fisher, *The Church of Christ in Yale College*, p. 72.

[3] *Ibid.*, p. 75.

[4] Abiel Holmes, *The Life of Ezra Stiles*, p. 34.

[5] *Ibid.*, p. 54.

the younger, Stiles was informed that there were three parties which were pleased with Stiles's election as president of Yale College. One was a small group of Arminians; then a slightly larger group of New Divinity "Gentlemen," to which Edwards belonged; and the main body of Calvinistic ministers. Edwards added, however, that either the Arminians or the Calvinists would be "greatly disappointed" in him.[6] It turned out that the New Lights were the most disappointed.

In his *Diary*, Stiles recorded adverse sentiments.

In all Connecticut I have heard of but one Gentleman that disapproves the Choice, (& it should seem that from this extensive Inquiry I might perceive any considerable Dissatisfaction, which none of the Gentleman's Friends or Enemies have yet suffered me to perceive tho I have earnestly entreated them to shew it me) and he is the Hon. Col. Davenport of Stanford a Gentleman of Learning and great Merit. He says the Corporation have done wrong in electing me; they should have chosen Mr. Tutor Dwight. He is of the Council and against enlarging the College Funds, judging that smaller Colleges are more advantageous for Education than larger Seats of Learning.[7]

Though the New Divinity "gentlemen" probably saw no great objection to Stiles, yet Stiles himself had little use for them. Unlike his predecessor he did not feel disposed to join with them. It was he who called the Revival "the late period of enthusiasm." He claimed that the difficulties in the churches at New Haven, Carmel, and Farmington were due to New Divinity and rigid discipline. He had "no objection," he stated, "against the moral characters of their ministers, who are pious, conscientious men, but very fixed and conscientious in some novel peculiarities."[8]

One day he rode over to Bethlehem and preached for Bellamy, the New Light leader. As a result of a conversation

[6] Ezra Stiles, *Literary Diary*. II, 227.
[7] *Ibid.*, II, 231.
[8] *Ibid.*, III, 374.

5

with him he concluded that it was impracticable to try to work with that group. "They are determined," he wrote, "to coalesce with none that are not in heart 'New.' My idea is that all Calvinists should unite. But I find they require besides a Union in their Idea of the divine Moral Character with respect to several of their favorite eurekas which they hold the Christian world never knew anything of till since President Edwards's death. They are determined to pursue with the greatest Vigor the formation of a New Divinity Connexion and Sect as distinct from all the New England Churches." [9]

Stiles was particularly emphatic in his scorn of the New Divinity when he received a letter from the Rev. Samuel Hopkins on February 1, 1781. He recorded his reactions in four remarks:

Remark 1, Very lamentable is the state of Religion at Newport and particularly that they will not attend public worship. But 2, One occasion of this Negligence is Brother Hopkins' new divinity. He has preached his own Congregation almost away or into an Indifference— he has 50 or 60 more Families of his own Congregation in Town, and might easily command a good Assembly if his preaching was as acceptable as his moral Character:—my congregation in Town are 70 or 80 families and would gladly attend such Preaching as Dr. Owens or Dr. Dodderidges or Preachers of far lower Abilities provided they were ejusdem Farinae with the first Puritan Divines. 3. Altho' New Divinity preachers collect some large Congregations in some parts as Taunton, Middleboro', Abington, etc. yet their preaching is acceptable, not for the new Tenets, but for its containing the good old Doctrines of Grace, on which the new Gentlemen are very sound and clear and full. In other parts where the Neighboring Ministers generally preach the old Calvinistic Doctrines, the People begin to be tired with the incessant Inculcation of the unintelligible and shocking new Points, especially that an Unconverted Man had better be killing his father and mother than praying for

[9] *Ibid.*, III, 4, 5.

converting Grace; that true Repentance implies a Willingness and desire to be damned for the Glory of God; that we are to give God Thanks, that he has caused Adam to sin and involve all his Posterity in total Depravity, that Judas betrayed and the Jews crucified Christ; etc. etc:—that the Children of none but Communicants are to be baptized, etc.: that the Churches and Ministers are so corrupt and laodicean and have so intermixt with the world, that the new Divinity Churches and Ministers cannot hold Communion but must and do recede and sequester themselves from them. Hence in Harwinton a Majority it is said, but to be sure a considerable Body of the Church and Congregation, are become opposed to Mr. Perry and have begun an Altercation which will probably end in a Separation. Remark 4. I do not perceive on whom Mr. Hopkins has his Eye for a Professor of Divinity. But Mr. Fitch tells me that Mr. Hopkins spake of Mr. West of Stockbridge as a great Scholar, a great Divine and excellently qualified for such an Office, but he supposed the Corporation would not chuse him; he also mentioned Mr. Hart of Preston as a great Divine. I rather think he supposed Mr. West would be acceptable to the Scholars. But when it is said he would be willing to preach in College a year on Tryal I should rather think he meant some one else besides Mr. West or Mr. Hart.[10]

The apparent confusion among the New Divinity men was also sensed by the Presbyterian minister, Ashbel Green, who visited Dr. Hopkins and remarked concerning it:

He [Dr. Hopkins] acknowledged to me that there was something difficult and inexplicable in attempting to reconcile the divine agency and influence with perfect human liberty and accountableness, and in explaining how moral evil came into the universe, and how the evil thoughts and actions of creatures are reconcilable with the perfect moral purity and unblamableness of God. I told him that those who are called Moderate Calvinists complain that the new divinity men pretend that there is no difficulty in these subjects.

And Green added,

His [Hopkins'] love of metaphysics carries him out of real life; but he appears after all, to be a man of real and fervent piety. His congre-

[10] *Ibid.*, II, 504, 505.

gation is almost extinct, and I have had queries with myself whether his abstruse manner of preaching has not contributed to drive his people from him.[11]

Stiles was particularly delighted when an opportunity came to bespatter his theological opponents. In 1787, he wrote:

They [the New Divinity group] perceive some of the pillars are removed; President Edwards has been dead twenty-nine years, or a generation; Dr. Bellamy is broken down, both body and mind, with a paralytic shock, and can dictate and domineer no more; Mr. Hopkins still continues, but past his force, having been somewhat affected by a fit and nervous debilitation; Mr. West is declining in health, and besides, was never felt so strong rods as the others. It has been the (Ton) [custom] to direct students in divinity, these thirty years past, to read the Bible, President Edwards, Dr. Bellamy, and Mr. Hopkins' writings: and this was a pretty good sufficiency of reading. . . . The very New Divinity Gentlemen say they perceive a disposition among several of their brethren to struggle for preeminence; particularly Dr. Edwards, Mr. Trumbull, Mr. Smalley, Mr. Judson, Mr. Spring, Mr. Robinson, Mr. Strong of Hartford, Mr. Dwight, Mr. Emmons, and others. They all want to be Luthers. But they will none of them be equal to those strong reasoners, Pres. Edwards and Mr. Hopkins.[12]

Stiles made it clear that he did not intend to spend his days in the fire of party struggle. "At most," he said, "I shall resist all claims and endeavors for supremacy or precedency of any sect." [13] He was consistent in this attitude when dealing with young Timothy Dwight, who threatened to seize Yale college for the New Divinity group.[14]

Meanwhile the battle against irreligion and the forces seeking to corrupt the church led Stiles increasingly to defend both Old and New Divinity against the growing liberal-

---

[11] J. H. Jones, *Life of Ashbel Green*, p. 239.
[12] G. P. Fisher, *The Church of Christ in Yale College*, p. 81.
[13] *Ibid.*, p. 79.
[14] Ezra Stiles, *Diary*, II, 531.

ism. "And I make no doubt," he claimed, "instead of the controversies of Orthodoxy and Heresy, we shall soon be called to the defence of the Gospel itself. At Home the general grand dispute is on the Evidence of Revelation—some few of your small folks indeed keep warming up the old Pye, and crying Calvinism, Orthodoxy, etc.—these are your Whitefields, Romaines, etc. that make a pother. . . . The Bellamys, etc. of New England will stand no Chance with the corruptions of Deism which, I take it, are spreading apace in this Country." [15]

The battle became open and vigorous under Dwight. His election as president of Yale gave the New Divinity group a strong and dynamic leader in an influential position. The chief strength of his Calvinistic faith, however, came not from the Congregationalists in New England but from the Presbyterians of New Jersey and other points south.

Ezra Stiles complained that in 1771, "an enterprising young Presbyterian from the Jersies" had settled in Salem and was trying

to assimilate the New England churches to Presbytery, and to render himself important by erecting a new system within our churches, under the pretext of guarding them against erroneous doctrines. Men in all ages have endeavored to aggrandize themselves on the Ruins of the Churches liberties. The plan of this Consociation is briefly, that it consist of the Pastors and one Messenger delegated from each church; to begin with three or more churches . . . they not to have Liberty to apply to or call in any other: to license candidates, etc. This transfers the power out of each distinct church and renders all subordinate to a Judicatorial Policy never suggested by Christ—and that on a principle upon which one might ascend to the all comprehensive and all absorbing Policy of the Pontificate. I am apprehensive this Salem Witchcraft may prevail.[16]

---

[15] I. W. Riley, *American Thought from Puritanism to Pragmatism*, p. 64.
[16] Ezra Stiles, *Diary*, I, 89.

There were a number of attempts made to adopt the Presbyterian form of church government in Massachusetts. But the response, on the whole, was rather feeble; in some cases, however, the opposition was so strong that the result was a failure. The Presbyterian churches in Massachusetts which were founded at this time died out except the one in Newburyport. Those Congregational churches which tried to adopt the Presbyterian form of church government were usually influenced by a desire to avoid the tax on the established church and declined when this motive no longer prevailed. Having thus embraced Presbyterianism "under the influence of circumstance, they had been reduced by circumstances to revert to their original form." [17]

In Connecticut the situation was different. After the Saybrook Platform was adopted the churches in that section of New England were for many years largely of Presbyterian character.[18] In fact, the terms Congregational and Presbyterian were used interchangeably. Whatever name was used, Presbyterianized-Congregationalism was the firmly established state religion, because the independence of the churches had been largely ruled out by the Saybrook Platform. It is

[17] William Hill: *History of Rise, Progress . . . of American Presbyterianism*, p. 57.
[18] On September 9, 1708, a group of twelve clergymen and four laymen assembled at Saybrook, Connecticut, summoned by the General Court, and adopted a platform of discipline in which it was stated "that the churches which are neighboring to each other, shall consociate, for mutual affording to each other such assistance as may be requisite upon all occasions ecclesiastical. And that the particular pastors and churches, within the respective counties in this government, shall be one consociation (or more, if they shall judge meet), for the end aforesaid." The General Court met October, 1708, and passed an act declaring "all the churches within this government, that are, or shall be, thus united in doctrine, worship, and discipline be, and for the future shall be owned and acknowledged established by law." From a copy of the minutes and records of the Saybrook synod and General Court in Benjamin Trumbull, *A Complete History of Connecticut*, I, 509–14 (Hartford, 1797). Ezra Stiles later referred to this as an "effort to presbyterianize the New England churches, by resolving all under ecclesiastical Judicatories." Stiles's *Diary*, I, 37.

not surprising, therefore, that these two ecclesiastical bodies increasingly coöperated. On November 5, 1766, the Consociated churches of Connecticut united with the Presbyterian Synod of New York and Philadelphia in the first annual convention, which was composed of Presbyterian delegates to the Synod, and of representatives from the Association in Connecticut. Later there was formed in the Yale Chapel

a meeting of delegates from General Assembly of Presbyterian churches and from General Association of Connecticut for Harmony; present Drs. Witherspoon, Rodgers, Mc Whorter, Mr. Tenant, Chapman, delegates from the Assembly, and Drs. Goodrich, Stiles, Edwards, Mr. Trumbull and Hart and Drs. Dwight, Rodgers, chairman, Dwight scribe. Agreed recommendation that two delegates be annually sent from General Assembly to sit in Assembly but without votes, and two delegates from Assembly to sit in General Association but without votes.[19]

Probably under the threat of a growing Episcopal sentiment as well as a latitudinarian sympathy, the Presbyterian form of church government was welcomed in Connecticut. Rather than see the power of the church of England established, the people of the Congregational faith assented to granting wider power to their elders and pastors.

Furthermore, the political and social complexion of the state favored this more centralized ecclesiastical organization. There were many families of standing and wealth who regretted the tendency to grant more and more power to the masses. A number of these families and leaders found themselves at home in the Episcopal church. If Congregationalists were to maintain their control they would have to adjust themselves and their religion to the trend of thought. These Federalists "preferred to concentrate power in the hands of the few, hesitating to trust the judgment of the

[19] Ezra Stiles, *Diary*, III, 431.

great body of citizens." [20] The result was that the leaders in the Congregational churches felt more and more kindly disposed toward the Presbyterian form of ecclesiastical government. Later this form of government proved valuable in helping to keep out the growing spirit of irreligion and deism. The fact that Unitarianism failed to get a foothold in Connecticut has often been attributed to the prompt and concerted action made possible by the Consociations.

Jonathan Edwards, the younger, further illustrates the coöperation and contact of the Presbyterians with New England Congregationalism. His illustrious father died while Jonathan was still a young child. His mother's death, shortly after, left him to the mercy of his Presbyterian environment. He managed to get a grammar school education at Princeton and advanced training at the Presbyterian College of New Jersey. Thus he received a Presbyterian form of New Light doctrine. Soon after leaving college he entered upon the study of divinity with the Reverend Joseph Bellamy, the friend and correspondent of his father. Following this he became a tutor in Princeton College. His call to the Congregational church at White Haven, Connecticut, gave him recognition as one of the leaders of the New Divinity theology. President Dwight and Jedidiah Morse were among his pupils.

The disciplinary character of the New Divinity and the Presbyterian polity made compatible bedfellows. Increasingly the New Divinity "gentlemen" coöperated with the theologians to the south of them. Edwards's call indicated the apparent sympathy between his theology and the atmosphere of New England. Though everything was not smooth in the running of his church, Edwards maintained enough support to stay a number of years. In 1782, Stiles tells of attending

[20] J. H. Jones, *The Life of Ashbel Green*, p. 336.

a union lecture at Mr. Whittlesey's Meeting: "Mr. Edwards preached. He has been settled about 13 or 14 years here and never before preached in Mr. Whittelsey's Meeting before— such has been the Disaffection of the two churches. Now the three Presbyterian or Congregational Churches in Town unite for Sacramental Lecture." [21]

From the time that Timothy Dwight brought the New Divinity group into power at Yale we find a closer and closer coördination of the Congregationalists and Presbyterians. Dwight was more than once a delegate from the General Association of Connecticut to the General Assembly of the Presbyterian church.

The state of Connecticut was not quick to feel the pressure of liberalism. But when she did, she had a bulwark established against it—a sense of unity vouchsafed largely by her Presbyterianized church government and "moderate" doctrine.

[21] Ezra Stiles, *Diary*, III, 10.

CHAPTER II

JEDIDIAH MORSE'S EARLY ENVIRON-MENT AND COLLEGE DAYS

INTO this complex ecclesiastical setting Jedidiah [1] Morse was born. His father, Deacon Morse of Woodstock, Connecticut, "held about all the offices in the town that he could lawfully hold, and was deacon of the First Church for 43 years." [2] There is no record of the father's theological beliefs but an indication of them is gained from the fact that he stood by the First Church through theological controversies and was an effective leader in restoring peace. The Woodstock church had been established in orthodoxy but its first pastor, Josiah Dwight (of the so-called Standing Order), who believed in the Cambridge Platform, was "suspected of theological loose-ness and, besides many idiosyncrasies, was accused of specu-lating in the wild lands of Killingly." [3]

This seemed to be the beginning of a turbulent career for the church. When Abel S. Stiles was called to the pastorate it was soon regrettably discovered that he was liberal in his viewpoint.

The fact that Mr. Stiles was a graduate of Yale College instead of Harvard, as his two predecessors had been, and his family connections were all with Connecticut, his parishioners were led to believe that he would favor the "Saybrook Platform" of faith, rather than the "Cam-bridge Platform," and if there was one thing our ancestors abhorred

[1] Sometimes spelled "Jedediah."
[2] C. W. Bowen, *Woodstock: an Historical Sketch*, p. 56.
[3] *Ibid.*, p. 36.

14

quite as much as Episcopacy or popery it was the "Saybrook Platform." To be tainted with that form of faith, as was the case with Mr. Stiles, after his settlement in Woodstock, was heresy indeed, and Woodstock was determined, according to her grant of 1683, to have none other but "an able, orthodox, godly minister." Instead of attending the Association of Ministers in Massachusetts, Mr. Stiles preferred the meetings of the Windham County Association in Connecticut. . . . Let it be said that there were two parties in the controversy, one side sympathizing with Mr. Stiles in his (more liberal) theological views, and the other side at first insisting on a minister who should conform in all respects to the "Standing Order" and afterwards opposed to Mr. Stiles personally as well as theologically.[4]

It is interesting to note that the Stiles party had favored, while the anti-Stiles party had opposed, the annexation of Woodstock to Connecticut. As a result of this controversy there was a break in the church and Stiles with his followers formed the Third, or North, Church of Woodstock.

The reaction to this dissension was an increase of the conservative attitude in the old First Church. When young Yale graduates appeared as candidates for the vacant pulpit they did not satisfy the congregation. The members finally agreed on a Harvard graduate, Abiel Leonard. In 1763, he was installed and "liquors, lemons and sugar provided for this joyful occasion gave equal satisfaction." [5]

The elder Jedidiah Morse was installed shortly after this as deacon in the church. He supported the new pastor in a somewhat liberal attitude. This was evident from the fact that in the following years the breach with the Third Church and Mr. Stiles was healed. A resolution was passed in the North Church stating:

Whereas the Pastor and church in North Woodstock have proposed to the Pastor and church in South Woodstock, that said South in terms

---

[4] *Ibid.*, pp. 39–40.
[5] E. D. Larned, *History of Windham County*, II, 98.

explicit should signify their Esteem of said Pastor and church in the North as in regular Ecclesiastical and Ministerial Standing, with their purpose of conducting towards them as such, engaging thereupon to do the same toward the Pastor and church in said South . . . that this should put an End to all Differences subsisting between them by a mutual Forgiveness of all officers and a Christian Deportment for the future. . . . Ratification of which, we the Pastor and Brethren of the North church, renewedly note to overlook and forgive all that has been offensive to us in the South church: engaging for the future to conduct towards them as becomes a church in Christian fellowship. Attested, Abel Stiles, Pastor.[6]

A similar resolution was framed and adopted by the members of the old First Church.

The liberal trend in Deacon Morse's church grew to such a point that instead of dissatisfaction with Yale candidates, a graduate of that institution, Eliphalet Lyman, was selected to fill the pastoral vacancy in the year 1777. It was also during this period that Mr. Leonard "met with the Presbytery and had the honorary title of Doctor of Divinity conferred upon him [at Princeton]." [7]

These events were characteristic of the attitude of the church in which young Jedidiah was born and grew in stature and in wisdom. The atmosphere and environment in which he received his early religious training were that of a sturdy, increasing liberalism. "No men in Woodstock were more respected and useful at this period than the deacons of the south church—William Skinner and Jedidiah Morse—who, with their popular pastor, are also reported as "the largest and finest looking men in the parish." Nor were the wives of these excellent men less respected and honored, but, we find, were rather regarded "as models of domestic virtues and Christian graces." Of one of them we read that "Certain

[6] *Ibid.*
[7] E. D. Larned, *Historical Gleanings of Windham County, Connecticut,* p. 122.

bright little boys then growing up in the families of Deacon Morse and Doctor Holmes may have received their first impulse to geographical and scientific studies from the teachings of this gifted and intelligent woman [Mrs. Jemima Bradbury]," [8] who was "endowed with superior natural and acquired abilities and power of mind . . . excelling in the doctrines of religion, in history, in natural philosophy and geography." [9] Further: "An abundant hospitality prevailed in Woodstock. Husking and apple-paring 'bees' and carding parties were popular. Spinning matches were reported in Boston and New London papers." [10]

Deacon Morse's sympathy must have been with Connecticut and Yale College or he would never have permitted his eighteen-year-old son Jedidiah to enter the institution at New Haven. It is entirely possible that young Jedidiah became acquainted with the newly elected president, Ezra Stiles, when the latter frequented his Uncle's pulpit in the North Woodstock Church. Inasmuch as Deacon Morse had been instrumental in healing the breach between the First and Third churches we may assume that he was not dogmatically opposed to the liberal tendencies of Abel Stiles and his nephew Ezra.

In the year 1779, young Jedidiah began his studies at the college. It was a period referred to as "the Dark Age of American Christianity." The enthusiasm and energy of the people had gone into the struggle for liberty, and an interest in personal religion was lacking. President Green of the Presbyterian College at Princeton stated that "there was nothing in Nassau Hall that had the appearance or name of religious revival." Religion was at a low ebb at Yale. It was

[8] E. D. Larned, *History of Windham County*, II, 106, 107.
[9] C. W. Bowen, *The History of Woodstock*, p. 135.
[10] *Ibid.*, p. 135.

17

said that the only reason many of the students attended the college was the fact that they would escape being drafted.[11] Jedidiah Morse's father had appealed to Governor Trumbull and had procured for his son "an exemption from military duty, so that he was enabled at once to take his place in college." [12] However, Stiles denied that this attitude was prevalent. In his *Diary* he recorded that out of the 224 students in the college (1781), "we cannot judge that a dozen have been brought to the college by this motive and that all the rest would have come to College had there been no war." [13]

Yale was largely dominated at this time by the intellect and personality of its president. The Professor of Divinity had not as yet been chosen and the task of instructing the students in theology was taken over by Dr. Stiles until Dr. Wales relieved him in 1782. Thus it was that Jedidiah Morse came under the influence of Stiles's complacent religion and conservative rationalism. That the young student's eager mind was impressed is evident in a letter he wrote home to his parents on January 6, 1782:

It is a matter of the greatest astonishment to me that mankind—made rational Beings, capable of distinguishing between good and evil—with the additional advantage of Divine Revelation—who are conscious to themselves that they are accountable Creatures—and on the least reflection must feel themselves exposed to everlasting destruction—I say after all these advantages and warnings, that they will go on in such a careless, heedless manner like irrational Beings, that they will be so easily seduced by the charms and allurements of this world, which, in itself considered, is as vain and worthless as those deluded Persons, who put their confidence in the enjoyment of it.

But a personal concern for the implications of the Calvinistic doctrine of Morse's background soon came to the fore. In

[11] J. B. Reynolds, *Two Centuries of Christian Activity at Yale*, p. 43.
[12] W. B. Sprague, *Life of Jedidiah Morse*, p. 2.
[13] Stiles, *Diary*, II, 564.

this same letter he continued more in the vein of New Light enthusiasm:

These cannot be matters of mere speculation; they are realities of eternal importance. The greatest enemy mankind has to encounter is his own corrupt heart. This invincible enemy, as to us, can only be conquered by Him who formed it. May my most earnest solicitations at the throne of Grace, be for this end that he would subdue my stubborn and perverse will and bring it into conformity to his own sovereign pleasure and for this end I desire your prayers in private as well as public.[14]

One of Morse's classmates, Payson Williston, wrote of him later:

I remember Morse, when he came to college, as a young man of dark complexion and dark eyes, with a more than commonly intellectual face, that easily lighted up into a smile. He had a fair reputation as a scholar, and was distinguished not more for good talents than for vigorous application. It was perhaps a fault in his character that, by the steady contemplation of an object, he would sometimes gain an exaggerated estimate of its importance, and that he would hold to it with an unyielding tenacity where a cooler judgment might have led him to relax.[15]

It is evident that Morse was sensitive and solemn. His temperament and nature fed on the New Light Calvinism. While still a boy of eighteen he wrote from college to his father and mother: "I stand in great need of them [the prayers of his parents] amidst thousands of temptations, where scarcely anything is to be heard, but cursing and swearing and taking God's name in vain. There are some in our class which use such language in all their discourse. I desire therefore, that you would intercede at the throne of Grace for me, that God would lead and direct me in the path of

[14] Letter, in Yale Collection of "Family Papers of Jedidiah Morse," Jan 6, 1782.
[15] W. B. Sprague: *Annals of the American Pulpit,* II, 251.

life and keep me from all temptations to sin. So I conclude, subscribing myself your dutiful and obediant son." [16]

Stiles's interpretation of religion did not stimulate great enthusiasm. Both personally and as an educator he had a distaste for the emotional expressions of religion. He felt that a rational appeal would produce the necessary, permanent results. But such results were not forthcoming. And yet, in spite of his cold, formal, and learned lectures a few students responded to him. His intellectual ability, no doubt, was a great attraction to some students. Jedidiah was one of the few who reacted to his teaching in the brief revival of 1781–83. After meeting with Dr. Stiles a number of times he wrote home:

It was always with the greatest Degree of Pleasure that I assumed my Pen to write to you; but if it can be increased, it is now, and intermixed with great anxiety; as I have something to inform you of, that is of the most importance to me, and of no small consequence to each of you. It is no less than a solemn Dedication of myself to God my Creator! Oh Dreadful Pleasing thought, it is an awful thing to transact with the living God—I hope I am in some measure sensible of it. I wish I may be more so—I was with the President and Holmes likewise, on Saturday and Sunday noon, when we gave our assent to be propounded and accordingly we were after the Service was over; the President gave us very good advice, read us the Confession of Faith, and the Covenant; he asked us many Questions and whether there were any Sentences in either the Covenant, etc. which we would not fully assent to, and as there were none, he replied that he should proceed to admit us a fortnight hence. And now my Dear Parents, I have need of your advice and Instructions but since I am deprived of your advice, I hope I am not of your Prayers. I can now call to mind the many profitable Instructions you have so often repeated to me and I have reason to reproach myself for paying so little regard to them. How can I better repay you for all your trouble and concern for me from my infancy than by giving myself to that God that made me, methink I can do it with the grateful Degree of Pleasure and

[16] Yale Letter, Nov. 28, 1779.

Satisfaction, and an humble Dependence on Jesus Christ the Mediator, and I pray that it may be done in a manner acceptable and well pleasing to him. I feel a secret inexpressible Pleasure arising in my Breast—mingled with a certain awe and reverence of God—I hope and trust I have an interest in the merits of a Crucified Saviour and that I have a desire to forsake all and follow him and embrace him as he is offered in the Gospel. May I be enabled to persevere in the solemn and important business which I am about to undertake. Oh that I might have clearer views of Christ and the way of Salvation by him, may I devote myself to him soul and body without reserve and be enabled to renounce all Sin, and may I be assisted by the Grace of God to withstand Temptation, and may I honour God and the Profession, and not make a mock of Divine Things—above all may I be enabled to put my whole trust and confidence in the Lord Jesus as the only hope set before me in the Gospel, and may all the Glory redound to [the] Holy Ghost.

And Morse concluded his letter with a comment on the religious situation of the college: "Religion seems to be flourishing in this Academy and it is to be hoped that God has begun a Good Work here and I desire that it may be carried on; Several Worthy characters seem to be seriously impressed with Divine Things and think it not a vain thing to serve the Lord." [17]

This revival was well received by Dr. Stiles. "Praise be God," he wrote, "I have reason to hope the blessed Spirit hath wrought effectually on the hearts of sundry, who have, I think, been brought home to God; and experienced what flesh and blood cannot impart to the human mind." [18] But the revival was short-lived. It did not strike fire in the student body as a whole but was merely a response of a few individuals. It may have been, however, that a number of students became connected with the churches to which their parents and friends belonged and the college records of con-

[17] Yale Letter, Feb. 20, 1781.
[18] Abiel Holmes, *Life of Ezra Stiles*, p. 278.

fession of faith would not be an accurate indication of interest in the church and religion.[19]

In less than a year, Morse gave a very different picture of religion at the college. He wrote again to his parents stating that "religion in this otherwise flourishing Society is at a low ebb—I wish it was in my power to inform you otherwise. We know not what the Determinations of Providence are concerning us. We hope for the best—we know all things will terminate finally in the greatest good. We aught to submit to the Decision of Providence with the most profound reverence and humility. Yet not withstanding these discouragements I have reason to hope there are a happy few who have not bowed the knee to Baal, who are reserved to do eminent service in the period of universal depravity—and who, I hope are constant in their supplication at the throne of Grace, for the effusion of his Holy Spirit on our land in general, and this society in particular." [20]

The studies required by the students of this period reveal some of the theological influences to which young Morse was exposed.[21] Stiles noted that the Senior class had "syllogistic Disputation, Forensics, Locke, and Vincent." [22] "Yesterday I put the Senior class into Pres. Clap's Ethics or Moral Philosophy. It was printed just before his death, and has been sometimes recited by the classes. Afterwards Pres. Edwards

[19] See Goodrich, "Revivals of Religion in Yale College," *Journal of American Educational Society*, Feb., 1838, p. 293.

[20] Yale Letter, Jan. 6, 1782.

[21] See Mary Latimer Gambrell, *Ministerial Training in 18th Century New England*.

[22] See Stiles, *Diary*, III, 99. The catechism (explicatory catechism of the Assembly's Shorter Catechism) taught by Stiles was written by the Rev. Thomas Vincent, sometime minister of Maudlin Milk Street in London. This book went through a number of editions. The Presbyterians published a copy in which it is noted, "Vincent's explanation of the Shorter Catechism has always been held in high estimation in the Presbyterian church, for its exact, full and scriptural illustration of that admirable summary of Christian doctrine and practise." See copy of Presbyterian Board of Publication (no date).

on the Will was recited; this giving offense was dropped." [23]

While Morse was at Yale the college still suffered from a certain unpopularity aroused during President Clap's administration. His attempt to maintain the orthodoxy of the institution had been strongly resisted. His efforts to stem the rising tide of New Light enthusiasm had not met with favor in many influential circles. When Stiles was elected president his sane rationalism was felt to be an adequate weapon to overcome this sentiment. Stiles's first act of renouncing the religious test inaugurated by Clap was hailed as a step in regaining confidence in the college.

But the New Divinity group was not satisfied. There was a constant and increasing friction between Stiles and Timothy Dwight. New Light sentiment was rapidly being changed from complacency and conflict with Old Calvinists, to a struggle against the French thought which the War had helped to introduce. This conflict was not open when Morse was a student, but the sources were present. What coöperation there was between Stiles and the New Divinity group was inspired largely by the president's desire to establish more full-time professorships. For this he needed money and many of the New Lights were influential and of the wealthy class. Consequently, we find him maintaining his friendship with a number of this group. On one Lord's Day in 1779, he preached for Jonathan Edwards the younger, when that divine was taken ill.[24] The following year he "attended Whitehaven all day," and heard Mr. Edwards preach on "the doctrine of Justification which he handled well." [25] When his wife died, Mr. Edwards had Dr. Stiles preach the funeral sermon.

[23] Stiles, *Diary*, II, 349.
[24] *Ibid.*, 362.
[25] *Ibid.*, 407.

Furthermore, Stiles coöperated with the revivalistic Presbyterians to the south of him. When John Brainerd, pastor of the Presbyterian church at Deerfield, New Jersey, died, Stiles pointed out that "he was a classmate of mine. He was not great in preaching tho' a pious, sound Divine; but exceedingly edifying in Conversation. He was a Trustee of Nassau Hall." [26] Later the Presbyterian, Dr. Rodgers, sent Stiles a proposal for a Concert of Prayer "for the Effusion of Good Spirit and Revival of Religion in the Lord." [27] In numerous ways the Presbyterians made an effort to work with the Congregationalists. Nassau Hall and the University of Edinburgh conferred a Doctor of Divinity degree upon the president of Yale as well as upon the Harvard president.[28] At the same time, Stiles indicated his attitude by writing:

It is one glory of a Presbyterian to be catholic and benevolent; it is another glory to stand fast in the faith. Many do not stop at the distinction between being charitable to another sect, and joining it. I may have charity for, and a good opinion of, a Lutheran; I may have a better for a Calvinist, and yet be, strictly, neither. I may have a good opinion of, and Christian affection for, all Protestant churches; I may have a very good opinion of those of Geneva and Holland; but perhaps, best of all for that of Scotland, or for those of New England.[29]

In a letter to a friend in Philadelphia Stiles wrote:

"It is of great importance, that the Presbyterian and Congregational interests be strongly united. Plans of union and harmony are greatly to be desired and promoted." [30]

In this environment the mind of young Morse expanded. His future sympathy with the Presbyterians, which had its birth in his Connecticut-Congregational-Presbyterian envi-

[26] Stiles, *Diary*, II, 530.
[27] *Ibid.*, III, 233.
[28] Ebenezer Baldwin, *History of Yale College*, p. 130.
[29] Abiel Holmes, *Life of Ezra Stiles*, pp. 78, 79.
[30] *Ibid.*, p. 73.

24

ronment, developed rapidly at the New Haven college; particularly because the New Haven institution was increasingly influenced by the New Light Presbyterian sentiments. By continuing his intense theological training after graduation Morse further strengthened these sentiments under the tutelage of Jonathan Edwards the younger. His attitude is reflected in another parental letter. "I pursue my studies slowly under the direction of the Rev. Dr. Wales, and Mr. Edwards. I am highly delighted with the study. I want nothing so much as to be able to attend to it without interruption." [31] In the opening of this letter the New Divinity emphasis is apparent. "No motive but Duty and a desire to promote the highest Interests of Mankind would ever induce me to be a preacher. These are motives abundantly sufficient. As for the esteem and applause of the world, I despise them when they come in competition with Duty. You are by this time assured, I hope, that I am determined to spend my life, my abilities and my all in the glorious Cause of the King of Kings." [32]

[31] Yale Letter, April 11, 1784.
[32] Ibid.

CHAPTER III

SETTLEMENT

W HILE pursuing his theological studies, Morse also engaged
in teaching a school of young girls in New Haven. It was
during this time that he realized the need for more adequate
geographical information relating to this country. As a result
he gathered all the information he could and compiled it in
the form of lectures to his school. Other schools felt the need
of similar information so that Morse was led to publish his
lectures in 1784, entitling them: *Geography Made Easy.*
This was the first geography to appear in America and its
author has often been called "The Father of American Geography." So enthusiastic was the reception of this work that
Morse was inspired during the rest of his career to devote a
great deal of his time and energy to future revisions and
similar works. The success of his geographical pursuits was
destined to have a very significant part in his theological
controversies. It opened the way to his acceptance by the educated, cultured, and often liberal groups in New England.
His correspondence and contacts brought him intimate relations with a number of influential scholars both in this
country and abroad. His numerous journeys in quest of information gave him a firsthand knowledge of the sentiments
of the nation. Undoubtedly his successful geographical labors
set for him a practical course of action rather than a speculative course of theological musing.

The disciplinary emphasis of his Calvinistic religion drew
young Morse into the active ministry. In 1785 he was exam-

ined and licensed to preach by the New Haven County Association after which he supplied the pulpit at Norwich, Connecticut, until he undertook the work of a tutor at his Alma Mater. Stiles, the president, made the following note: ". . . I introduced Mr. Morse, who was elected Tutor at Hartford on Election Day, and gave him the Tuition of the Freshmen." [1]

But the young tutor's health was so frail that it soon became necessary for him to give up his work at the college. At the same time his classmate, Abiel Holmes, pastor of a Congregational church in Midway, Georgia, had "returned to New England to escape, for a time, the enervating influence of a Southern climate; and the two friends agreed with the consent of the College Faculty, that they would temporarily exchange places and occupations, with a view to their mutual benefit." [2] Stiles indicated that health was not the only consideration in Morse's proposed change. "Mr. Morse, desiring to be absent while [during] Spring in order to make the Tour of the States to Georgia for perfecting a new edition of his Geography, we elected the Rev. Abiel Holmes, Tutor." [3]

In preparation for this trip south Morse was ordained along with Samuel Austin on the 9th of November, 1786. "After opening the Council Mr. Tutor Morse asked ordination also with a View to his travels thro' the southern states. We examined the candidates. . . ." [4] At the services which followed, Edwards delivered "an excellent sermon from Acts 20:26, 'I am pure from the blood of all men. . . .'" and Morse commented that "the whole services were performed with great propriety and solemnity." [5] "Prayer by Mr. Wil-

---

[1] Stiles, *Diary*, III, 228.
[2] Sprague, *Life of Jedidiah Morse*, p. 8.
[3] Stiles, *Diary*, III, 244.
[4] *Ibid.*, p. 246.
[5] Sprague, *Life of Jedidiah Morse*, p. 9.

liston, Imposition of Hands by Messrs. Whitt'ly, Williston, Edwards, Street and myself," wrote Stiles. "Mr. Whitt'ly gave the charge; then Mr. Holmes came up into the Pulpit and gave the right hand of Fellowship, Mr. Lockwood made the concluding Prayer, and Mr. Austin [6] gave the psalm and Blessing. Three Hours exercise." [7]

Morse left immediately for Midway, Georgia, where, during his brief stay, he made many contacts of value for his *Geography* and for his future theological activities. Among the latter were a number of Presbyterians whose influence was to be of lasting importance to the young preacher. The following year he was back at Yale where Stiles wrote of him: "I attended and heard the Rev. Mr. Morse preach at Chapel all day. . . . Two ingenius and excellent sermons. Mr. Morse resides in Town, lives at Dr. Wales, perfecting a new edition of his Geography, and in a few months [is] to go and preach at Elizabethtown in Jersey." [8]

It is quite likely that Morse was drawn to preach in Elizabethtown by the attraction of a young lady, whom he met in New York at the home of his Presbyterian friend, Ebenezer Hazard, a member of the United Presbyterian church of that city. Elizabethtown was not far from Shrewsbury, New Jersey, the home of Miss Elizabeth Ann Breese, daughter of Samuel Breese, Esq., and granddaughter of Dr. Samuel Finley, president of the Presbyterian College at Princeton. [9] This friendship, which eventuated in marriage on May 14, 1789, was to cement the ties of Morse to the leaders of the

[6] It is interesting to note that Mr. Austin was later known as one of the leading New Lights. In fact, at the installation of Dr. Dana in the New Haven First Church in 1789, only three years later, the "only decided New Divinity men were Dr. Edwards and Mr. Austin." See Leonard Bacon's *Historical Discourse*, New Haven, 1839, p. 275.

[7] Stiles, *Diary*, III, 246, 247.

[8] *Ibid.*, p. 291.

[9] See W. B. Sprague, *Life of Jedidiah Morse*, p. 15, and S. I. Prime, *Life of S. F. B. Morse*, p. 6.

Presbyterian church. In fact, shortly before his marriage, he was preaching for some months as a candidate in the Presbyterian church in New York City. This church was divided in sentiment between Morse and another candidate.[10] Hazard wrote that Morse "is undoubtedly a man of genius; but among us he did not do himself justice. His Geography employed (he thought necessarily) so much of his time, that he could not devote enough to his theological studies, and thus injured himself in the opinion of some, who, I am sure, would have been fond of him, could he have studied more." [11]

The factors which resulted in Morse's settlement at the First Church in Charlestown, Massachusetts, are very significant. It was during the time that Morse was preaching in the New York church that the Charlestown pulpit became vacant and Dr. Belknap of Boston wrote to his friend, Ebenezer Hazard, inquiring about their candidate. Hazard replied:

In a former letter, you asked my opinion of Mr. Morse as a preacher. I like him; and indeed, so far, he proves very well acceptable to our people in general. He composes well, has many new and striking ideas, and there is something pleasing in his manner. He wants animation, but probably will have more of it after he has been longer in the ministry, and is more used to the people and the houses in which he speaks, but particularly when he is more weaned from his manuscript. . . . In his doctrines, he is strictly Calvinistical. As a man, I am charmed with him. He is judicious and sensible, decent and modest in his deportment, a chearful companion, who prettily supports the dignity of the clergyman in the midst of friendly affability.[12]

This was the beginning of an effort made by Belknap and Hazard to get their candidate located in the Charlestown

---

[10] James Muir, "a Scotch minister from Bermuda."
[11] Yale Letter, Nov. 15, 1788. (Printed in *Belknap Papers*, Part 2, Mass. Historical Society, 5th Series, III, 72–74.)
[12] *Ibid.*, III, pp. 30, 31.

church. In fact it was largely the influence of these two men that persuaded Morse that he should go to that church and that led the Charlestown people to be favorable to Morse. Frequently these two men spoke of Morse as "our author." [13] "I have a very sincere regard for him," wrote Hazard to Belknap, "and wish the Charlestown people may be unanimous in their call to him; for I am persuaded they will not do better, and I wish him to have satisfactory evidence that it is his duty to go there." [14]

Hamilton Andrew Hill in his history of the Old South Church claimed that Morse "received the call to Charlestown through the influence of Mr. Belknap, with whom he had much in common in his taste for geographical and historical studies." [15] However, Belknap alone could not have accomplished this settlement. It was his union with the Presbyterians, with whom candidate Morse was also in sympathy, that consummated the final arrangements. It was claimed that

some of the Congregational ministers were gradually Presbyterianizing the denomination, by the introduction and adoption of methods designed to limit and embarrass the free action of the churches in their choice and settlement of pastors, thus undermining the very foundation principles of Congregationalism. . . . In one respect, however, there had been a steady divergency from the old Congregational way, to what about this time became a fixed usage, namely, the examination and certified approval of candidates for the sacred office, by clerical associations. . . . Letters of commendation from experienced pastors, which a young minister would naturally take when going among the churches as a candidate, gradually assumed the form and authority of credentials, till, in 1790, the convention of Congregational ministers virtually made them necessary, by recommending that only those bearing such papers from clerical bodies be admitted to the pulpits.

[13] *Ibid.*, p. 120.
[14] *Ibid.*, p. 73.
[15] H. A. Hill, *History of the Old South Church*, II, 245.

Thus the business of testing the qualifications of a young man for the ministry silently and gradually passed from the churches to the clergy, where the sole responsibility now rests.[16]

In line with this policy, Belknap enlisted the influence of Joshua Paine of Sturbridge, a former pastor of the Charlestown church. He also secured the help of Richard Cary, one of the leaders in the Charlestown church and a member of the Parish committee. Cary replied to Belknap in a letter dated November 21, 1788: "Freedom in friendship adds to the pleasures of it. As you are sensible, my endeavors will not be wanting to obtain Mr. Morse." [17] Likewise, Cary wrote to Paine telling him that they had Mr. Morse preaching as a candidate and added:

Your recommendation greatly excited the desire of the people to hear him. . . . He discovers the pious Christian, as well as the judicious divine. His amiable, prudent, benevolent temper will always command him affection and esteem. He preached upon the great doctrines of the gospel in such a clear, evangelical strain as to engage the closest attention and admiration of the congregation. . . . His acceptance of it [the call] will greatly promote peace and harmony here, so essential to the prosperity of any people.[18]

Belknap reported to Hazard in New York that

Morse was well received at Charlestown. They kept him preaching almost every day, and sometimes twice a day, during his short stay; he preached three times in this town [Boston]. He appears to have an improvable mind and a good heart, and I believe will wear well. He will certainly have a call at Charlestown, and they say it will be unanimous.[19]

[16] J. S. Clark, *Historical Sketch of the Congregational Churches in Massachusetts*, p. 228.
[17] *Belknap Papers* (Massachusetts Historical Society, 6th Series, IV, 426).
[18] *Ibid.*, pp. 426, 427.
[19] *Belknap Papers*, Part 2 (Massachusetts Historical Society, 5th Series, III, 76).

When the church membership finally voted unanimously to accept him, Belknap, Hazard and Cary rejoiced. Cary wrote to the minister of the Federal Street church: "Harmony prevailed. . . . Now my friend, does not this give new occasion or add to our joy and thankfulness on the approaching day of thanksgiving—such a union in the parish and such a prospect of a good minister. Surely we can't be thankful enough to the great Head of the Church." [20] Meanwhile Morse accepted the call, stating, "The unanimity, the affection and the generosity manifested in the call, induce me and my friends to believe that it is the call of God, and that Providence is, by this means, pointing to Charlestown as the scene of my future ministerial labours." [21]

On April 30 of the following year, the Installing Council met to examine and to receive this newcomer to the Boston vicinity. The following clergymen and delegates from their churches were present: Joseph Jackson of Brookline; Joshua Paine of Sturbridge; Timothy Hilliard of Cambridge; David Osgood of Medford; Jeremy Belknap, Peter Thacher, John Eliot and Joseph Eckley of Boston; and Eliphalet Lyman of Morse's home church in Woodstock, Connecticut. Dr. Belknap preached the sermon on the text: "Neither as lording it over God's heritage; but as ensamples to the flock," from I Peter 5:3. Belknap sent a copy of the sermon to his friend John Adams, Vice President of the United States, who replied that he had met Morse and that he "appears to be an interesting character, and a man of literary merit"; and in respect to the sentiments of Belknap's address he remarked: "the more the subject is considered, the sooner all men will be convinced that human passions are all insatiable; that, instead of being extinguished, moderated or contested, they

[20] *Belknap Papers* (Massachusetts Historical Society, 6th Series, IV, 428).
[21] Sprague, *Life of Jedidiah Morse*, pp. 13, 14.

always strengthen by indulgence and gratification; and therefore the only security against them is in checks, whether in civil or ecclesiastical societies." [22]

The religious attitudes and sentiments of many of those who participated in Morse's Installing Council are important in the light of future events. Belknap, as already indicated above, had decided leanings toward the Presbyterians. He was pastor of the Federal Street church in Boston, which previously had been Presbyterian—it was founded by John Moorhead and a group of Irish farmers. While on a visit in 1785 to Philadelphia, Belknap "attended divine worship at the 'Scots Seceders' Church; in the afternoon, he preached for Mr. Duffield, pastor of the old Presbyterian Society, and remaining in the city through the next week, he preached on the next Sabbath for Dr. Ewing and Dr. Sprout, also Presbyterian clergymen." [23] He observed that "the Presbyterians in this part of the country seem to be forming a union, and laying aside their former distinctions: this is another good sign." [24]

Mr. Eckley, of the Old South Church in Boston, was orthodox, with a Presbyterian background. He was graduated from Princeton in 1772, licensed to preach by the Presbytery of New York in 1776, and later received his Doctor of Divinity degree from the College of New Jersey. There is an indication that at this time Peter Thacher leaned toward the re-

---

[22] Sprague, *Life of Jedidiah Morse*, pp. 16, 17. Quoted also in Belknap's *Life* by his granddaughter, pp. 172, 173; and in the collection of *Belknap's Papers*.

[23] The *Life of Jeremy Belknap*, collected and arranged by his granddaughter, p. 116.

[24] *Ibid.*, p. 116. Belknap was considered a liberal according to Justin Winsor. "In 1778, a Unitarian minister was the agent in securing for the church (Charlestown), the services of that redoubtable champion of Orthodoxy, Rev. Dr. Morse, and preached his ordination sermon." Justin Winsor, *Memorial History of Boston*, III, 474. Winsor no doubt read back into history the word Unitarian, although all of the Boston ministers of that period were believed to have held the Unitarian sentiments.

vivalistic sentiment. "Whitefield, in reference particularly to the fervor of his prayers, called him 'the young Elijah,' and the strictness of his orthodoxy, not less than the depth and warmth of his devotion gave him great favor, especially with the more zealous portions of the religious community." [25] However, time was to bring a great change in the spiritual complexion of these ecclesiastical brethren and Thacher particularly became one of Morse's most energetic antagonists.

The unanimity and pleasure with which Morse was welcomed and installed seemed to indicate a bright future. Belknap's comment to Hazard expressed the feeling of the time: "Mr. Morse's installment was well conducted, and everyone seemed to be pleased. He has the character of an agreeable and growing man, and I am glad he is settled where he can have so many literary advantages as at Charlestown." [26]

[25] H. A. Hill, *History of the Old South Church*, II, 132.
[26] *Ibid.*, p. 245.

CHAPTER IV

JEDIDIAH MORSE AT CHARLESTOWN AND IN THE BOSTON ENVIRONMENT

"T H E whole atmosphere around him was eminently intellectual—the most cultivated society in Boston was always accessible to him; and the ministers of the Boston Association to which he belonged, received him with great cordiality, and he, in turn, gratefully reciprocated their expressions of good will. Dr. Belknap . . . for some time, his intimate friend . . . was always on the alert to promote the interests of his young brother in the ministry, by every means in his power." [1]

The Congregational atmosphere in Boston, as it might have impressed a Presbyterian, was reflected in a report by Ashbel Green of his visit to a meeting of the Boston Association in 1791:

About twelve o'clock I came over to Mr. Eckley's, with whom I am now to lodge. After dinner went to the Association of Clergy in and about Boston, and I was glad to see one of their meetings. They assemble once a fortnight in each other's houses by rotation. The time of meeting is three o'clock, P. M., but members are dropping in till five, and no account is required of causes of absence or delay. At four o'clock the chairman is expected to pray, but this part of the duty in the present instance fell on me as a stranger, and I performed it but poorly. The prayer is usually the only thing of a religious nature

---

[1] W. B. Sprague, *Life of Jedidiah Morse*, p. 22.

which claims attention. The meetings are indeed so frequent that there cannot be ecclesiastical concerns to occupy the time spent in them all. Yet I am ready to believe that there might be much useful conversation on religious subjects—on sentiments, doctrines, history, facts, etc., if the members were generally disposed to spend their time in this manner; much also, I conceive, might be employed in devising plans for the advancement of true religion, if the members of the Association were so disposed to spend their time. But, as I understand, they are so diverse in their sentiments that they cannot agree on any point in theology. Some are Calvinists, some Universalists, some Arminians, some Arians, and one at least is a Socinian. How absurd it is for men of such jarring opinions to attempt to unite. How much more conducive to improvement and to pleasure, that the parties should divide, and that those who are agreed should walk by themselves. Yet this plan I know would be esteemed by them as the effect of bigotry and narrowness of mind; and so they will meet, and shake hands, and talk of politics and science, and laugh, and eat raisons and almonds, and apples and cake, and drink wine and tea, and then go about their business when they please. To such a meeting as this, for the purposes of amusement, relaxation or sociability, few would probably object. But for the purposes of church government, to me, at least, it appears ludicrous. . . .[2]

William Bentley a few years later described his first visit to the Boston Association:

We had the ingenious Historian, Dr. Belknap, the lovely heretic, Dr. Howard, the pious Dr. Eckley, the elegant Dr. Clarke, the good Dr. Lathrop, the Geographer Dr. Morse, with the judicious Eliot, and the cautious West. After tea we had some agreeable conversation and the young Ladies of the family entertained us with vocal music as an accompaniment of the Forte Piano, upon which one of the Daughters performed very excellently. The amiable mother assisted them with her voice.[3]

Other aspects of the environment into which Morse was installed are dramatically portrayed in a letter published in

[2] J. H. Jones: *Life of Ashbel Green*, pp. 224, 225.
[3] William Bentley, *Diary*, II, 255.

1791, by a young French traveler, Jean Pierre Brissot de Warville. Upon his visit to this country, and Boston in particular, he commented:

> How I enjoyed the activity of the merchants, the artisans, and the sailors! . . . Everything is rapid, everything great, everything durable . . . Boston is just rising from the devastations of war, and its commerce is flourishing; its manufactures, productions, arts, and sciences offer a number of curious and interesting observations. . . . The Bostonians unite simplicity of morals with that French politeness and delicacy of manners which render virtue more amiable. . . . The excellence of this morality characterizes almost all the sermons of all the sects through the Continent. The ministers rarely speak dogmas: universal tolerance, the child of American independence, has banished the preaching of dogmas, which always leads to discussion and quarrels. All the sects admit nothing but morality, which is the same in all, and the only preaching proper for a great society of brothers. . . . Everyone at present worships God in his own way, at Boston. Anabaptists, Methodists, Quakers, and Catholics profess openly their opinions: . . . The ministers of different sects live in such harmony that they supply each other's places when any one is detained from his pulpit. . . . They have concluded that it is best to tolerate each other, and that this is the worship most agreeable to God.[4]

About this period Timothy Dwight, president of Yale College, wrote in his *Travels in New England,* that "the commerce of Boston is very extensive. . . . The liveliest impression that was ever made on my mind of cheerful activity has been communicated by the vast multitude of boats and larger vessels moored in this harbor or moving over its waters in a thousand directions. The wealth of Boston is great. Individuals have risen to high opulence in greater numbers, compared with the mass of population than in any other large town of the United States." Further observations shed light on the religious situation at the close of the eighteenth cen-

---

[4] *Old South Leaflets,* VI, 1–4.

tury. "During one hundred and forty years," he wrote, "Boston was probably more distinguished for religion than any city of the same size in the world. An important change has, however, within a period of no great length taken place in the religious opinions of the Bostonians. Before this period, moderate Calvinism very generally prevailed. At the present time, Unitarianism appears to be the predominating system. . . ." [5] This was the atmosphere of the New England into which Morse came, characterized as it was by a cultured seriousness, an energetic concentration upon commerce with its promise of great wealth, and the secularization of religion by its emphasis upon a benevolent system of morals.

William Bentley was probably the most outstanding representative of this temper. From the time that he began his ministry in the Salem church he found

in the commercial character of our people, much to satisfy the demands of his liberal and investigating mind, and consequently he readily assimilated with them. This blending of the peculiar elements which characterised pastor and people served to develop in Dr. Bentley those catholic and liberal views of Christianity, as well as those generous social virtues, for which he was so highly distinguished, and made him so popular as a Pastor.[6]

Bentley's religious sentiments were clearly expressed in his Stone Chapel Sermon. "When a man is found," he said, "who does not possess much, nor despise all, who is pure from guile, peaceable in his life, gentle in his manners, easily disuaded from revenge, with an heart to pity and relieve the miserable, impartial in his judgment, and without dissimulation, this is the man of religion. . . . Virtue alone is the moral happiness of the world, and personal virtue alone se-

[5] *Ibid.*, 226–43.
[6] Joseph G. Waters, "History of East Church," Introduction to Bentley, *Diary*, I, xi.

cures heaven." [7] It was natural that Bentley and James Freeman of King's Chapel in Boston, should be close friends: ". . . their college attachments ripened into a mutual fraternal affection, when their minds came into full harmony on matters of religious faith." [8] The liberal Salem pastor paid high tribute to his Unitarian brother. "I put the highest value upon this man as a gentleman and a Scholar, as a man of religion, with a pure life, of good opinions without obstinacy, and as the most liberal and judicious preacher of his times." [9]

There was also in Morse's environment a group of religious leaders called Hopkintonians or Hopkinsians. Their enthusiasm for evangelical and revivalistic religion was obnoxious to the conventional Boston preachers and to the cultured Bentley, who expressed his attitude thus:

It is our misfortune in Essex, to feel severely the consequences of measures adopted by men called Hopkintonians, whose leading maxim is to embitter the minds of men by the fear of dangerous delusions from all other men but themselves, having neither system nor reputation to support them. Spring is at their head in Newbury—and the only quiet one in his own congregation which is the smallest in Newburyport. Parish, in Newbury, is opposed by a Majority. Bradford at Rowley is not established by a Presbyterian ordination, and is an exceptionable character among his party. Hopkins of Salem is a cunning man. Spaulding a very weak one. Their Marblehead Society is at present lost after most unhappy dissensions. Cleveland of Ipswich is old, and of little consequence. In the parts of Middlesex bordering upon us these enthusiasts abound. Cleveland's Son, a Lieutenant in the Army, without education, is at Stoneham. At Reading they are preparing to settle one against a powerful opposition. Mr. Prentice must soon quit, as they have rendered him so unhappy by a party in his own parish. Judson has become uncomfortable at Malden who is one of these Schemers. Several clergymen of inferior abilities settled

---

[7] William Bentley's *Sermon Preached at Stone Chapel*, Boston, Sept. 12, 1790, pp. 9, 21.
[8] Bentley, *Diary*, I, xiv (Introduction).
[9] *Ibid.*, III, 36.

near them, are suffering from the exertions of this party. In truth we are in a religious ferment as to one part of the community near us, while in the other there is an abundant liberality in some, licentiousness in many others, and a few in different religious opinions, who lead quiet and peaceable lives in godliness and honesty. It is full time that the civil power should view all opinions as harmless, and that good men should by precept and example place the greatest stress upon sober maxims of life. A Hopkintonian is respectable if not uncharitable. There always has been a sect to whom uncharitableness seems particularly to have belonged. Once it was the Anabaptists but they have now risen to some importance and can subsist without it. It is now left to others, who are struggling to rise.[10]

A growing number of people were evidently being attracted to this "ultra-Calvinism" of the Hopkinsians by a conviction that religion was more than a reasonable system of morality. They felt the need of an emotional outlet for their religious faith and found it in this type of "enthusiasm." Among these people were rich and poor alike, but the majority were laborers, sailors, and immigrants to whom the aristocratic religion did not appeal.[11]

Then there was a middle group which was well educated and possessed many of the social graces of the liberals but which felt that true religion had its emotional expression along with its formal emphasis upon ethics. It was in this group of so-called Moderate Calvinists that Morse found his place. There were times, however, when he was identified with the other groups, for he had much in common with each one of them. When he emphasized his revivalistic tendencies he was branded a New Light and associated with the Hopkinsians. He was made the object of malevolent attacks by the liberals and labeled with such names as "knave, fool, ig-

[10] *Ibid.*, I, 160–61.
[11] See Bentley, *Diary*, for many references to this fact. The evidence does not reveal a sharp economic distinction between the orthodox and the liberals.

norant impostor." [12] The contempt which the liberals expressed for the New Lights was likewise heaped upon the Charlestown pastor. This will appear in our account of his controversy over the Illuminati and Harvard College. His association with his Boston friends and his fellow geographers led the Hopkinsians to mistrust him. In his attempts to found the theological seminary at Andover he had to fight against this attitude. These elements in his environment stimulated his sensitive nature in the spirit of controversy.

When he started out upon his ministerial career at Charlestown the words of Dr. Belknap's Installation Sermon were still ringing in his ears:

We have no reason to suspect that you will ever attempt to lord it over God's heritage; you will neither dogmatise in your preaching, nor be arbitrary in your conduct. You will preach what you believe to be the truth, and charge your hearers to judge of it by the same infallible oracles from which you derive your information. You will not puzzle them with metaphysical subleties, but will aim to feed them with the sincere milk of the word that they may grow thereby. To insist much on controverted points, may serve to feed a party-spirit; but is not good for the use of edifying. That preaching is generally the most successful, which is the most searching, the most spiritual, the most practical. We should aim directly at the heart; and endeavor to make men feel their concern in what we preach, and the most effectual way to do this, is to feel it ourselves. The truth, when it comes from the heart, will be likely to reach the heart.[13]

All indications pointed to a happy and prosperous ministry for the young preacher. "The people composing the parish of which he took charge, though generally of the middle and plainer class, were capable of appreciating the excellent qualities of their new Pastor, while there were among

[12] Manuscript in Essex Institute, Salem, Mass.: Letter to Bentley from F. Nichols, 1797, Nos. 55, 56.

[13] *Belknap's Sermon* at the Installation of Jedidiah Morse, p. 21.

them several distinguished for high intellectual culture, the finest moral and religious qualities, and a widely extended and most benign influence." [14] Mr. Osgood in addressing the Charlestown congregation at the installation called to their attention the fact that they had a pastor "whose mature age, opportunities for knowledge, and specimens already given, both of literary and moral improvement, are such as afford ground to hope for him distinguished usefulness." [15]

The distinction gained through the fame of his *Geography* immediately gave Morse entrance to the cultured and literary groups of Charlestown and Boston. Such was his interest in, and contact with this class that later an edition of *Chesterfield on Politeness, Improved by Dr. Morse,* was attributed to him. [16] When he and his young bride went to their parish they stayed at the home of Richard Cary, one of the most distinguished and wealthy citizens of the town. [17] Consequently, the aristocratic and newly rich of Charlestown welcomed Morse as one of their very own. At the same time the "middle and plainer classes" united with them in approbation of the new pastor. His strong evangelical and Presbyterian sentiments probably won them. The new minister's wife tactfully appealed to this group, for she remarked that she liked Charlestown because she could dress in calico. [18]

Morse set the course of his theological future without delay. Filled with the enthusiasm of a young Elijah he preached

[14] W. B. Sprague, *Life of Jedidiah Morse*, p. 21.

[15] See "Right Hand of Fellowship," printed with Belknap's sermon.

[16] See W. B. Sprague, *Life of Jedidiah Morse*, p. 3.

[17] Miss Lucy Osgood, who knew Morse well, describes him: "His tall, slender form, the head always slightly inclining forward, his extremely neat dress, mild manners, and persuasive tones, aided by the charm of that perfect good-breeding which inspires even the rudest with a sense of respect for the true gentle woman, made him in all places a most acceptable guest, while his own house was always celebrated as the very home of hospitality." Samuel I. Prime: *Life of Samuel F. B. Morse*, p. 7.

[18] See *Belknap Papers*, Part 2 (Massachusetts Historical Society, 5th Series, Vol. III).

the Sabbath after his installation on the text: "For I determined to know nothing among you, save Jesus Christ and Him Crucified." Then he turned to the practical means of promoting the interest of religion among his flock. He established a monthly lecture, using Watts and the Assembly's Catechism as the basis of instruction. Later monthly meetings in the town resulted in a quickening of the religious conscience and Morse's evangelical efforts seemed to be having an effect.

It was evident from the beginning of his ministry that his primary interest centered in the promotion of revivalistic religion. He threw his energy into every situation where he could advance this cause. In 1794 at Plymouth, he participated in a season of religious enthusiasm. Dr. Robbins, pastor of the church in that town thanked him for his help. "My family and people speak of your visit with great satisfaction; and I have abundant reason to believe your labours were not in vain in the Lord; for I have heard many speak of the sermons as blessed to their edification and consolation in Jesus Christ. I mention this to excite gratitude in your heart, as well as to encourage you in your Master's work." [19]

Furthermore, he utilized the ministerial custom of serving in turn at the Boston Thursday lectures, as an opportunity to stimulate his religious sentiments. Sprague states that Morse officiated fourteen times at this lecture in the four years after his installation at Charlestown.[20]

He was no doubt aroused to champion his beliefs by an anonymous letter from a layman, which challenged him to prove the divinity of Christ and to refute certain arguments. On December 30, 1789, a few months after his installation he wrote to his father stating: "I have been writing by par-

[19] W. B. Sprague, *Life of Jedidiah Morse*, p. 23.
[20] *Ibid.*, p. 25.

43

ticular desire of a Boston gentleman, a defence of the Divinity of the Saviour,—a doctrine that is denied by many. I have written twelve sheets upon the subject. I know not but I shall feel it my duty to publish." [21]

In his opening statement at the lecture he made the following declaration:

Convinced as I am of his Divinity, and that this is a fundamental truth of Christianity, I desire by every fair argument to convince others. As a disciple of Christ, as his ambassador—however unworthy of the honour—I am under indispensable obligations, as far as my knowledge and ability will admit, not only to inculcate his excellent moral precepts, and to illustrate and defend his doctrines, but especially to maintain his personal honour and dignity, and to assert and vindicate his Divinity. . . . When an article of faith of so much importance comes to be called in question, denied, laughed at, it behooves those who believe the doctrine to lend their seasonable aid for its maintenance. At such a time as this especially, its vindication cannot but be of service, by the Divine blessing, to the cause of truth. [22]

But the thunder of controversy was already rumbling behind the scenes. It was evident that the cultured, liberal pastors of Boston and vicinity were beginning to look with discontent upon this young revivalist, who constantly took it upon himself to champion evangelical religion. Bentley wrote in his diary on July 22, 1790, that "a Mr. Morse of Charlestown has begun a course of lectures upon the Trinity at the Thursday lecture. The clergy fear the controversy should be opened and yet the Orthodox will be meddling with it." [23] Sensing the influence which Morse was beginning to have in their section, these liberals were more and more concerned with his activities. They considered his labors for evangelical religion as an expression of great pride—and, to

[21] *Ibid.*, p. 50.
[22] *Ibid.*, p. 51.
[23] Bentley, *Diary*, I, 187.

say the least, uncharitable and unbecoming for one of his culture. All expressions of this type of religion were associated with the illiterate, itinerant preachers and the New Light extravagances.

When Morse published his *American Geography,* Bentley noted that it received a "severe lashing . . . for omission of Great Names in this state, and the free insertion of less distinguished names in Conn." [24] This also pointed to the fact that Morse's sympathies were still with his New Divinity friends of his home state. But the liberal sentiments of Boston and its environs were slowly crystallizing against him. "The Unitarian minister of King's Chapel," Bentley wrote, "has appeared against Morse's *Geography,* and the cause is contested with great party zeal." [25] The liberals knew that Morse owed much of his influence to his *Geography* and if they could but minimize the fame of that work its author would be speedily eclipsed. With an evident sense of satisfaction Bentley pointed out that his friend, Freeman "has published his remarks upon Morse's *Universal Geography,* which exposes that Geographer so fully to the World, as to lay his geographising abilities under suspicion; and perhaps they in the future will be in little demand." [26]

The immediate result upon such a character as Morse was to spur him on in his work, but the effects were far reaching. "Spent an hour," wrote Bentley, "with Thomas, the celebrated Printer who is not pleased that Mr. Freeman should check the sale of Morse's *Geography* when the copyright was entirely in his own hands, and when the supposed cause of offense, Morse's reflections on an altered copy of Watt's *Cradle Hymns,* made him also a sufferer." [27]

[24] *Ibid.,* II, 32.
[25] *Ibid.,* 70.
[26] *Ibid.,* 64.
[27] *Ibid.,* 71.

At first, the difference between these factions was not theological, but rather had its basis in sentiment. Morse had little cause to disagree with many of the gentlemen from Boston on the fundamental doctrines of religion—for the majority did not at this time follow the most liberal of the group. But he noticed the indifference toward what he considered vital in the Christian religion and the resultant laxness in religious enthusiasm among the people. Gradually the New England Calvinism was becoming secularized by the influence of the post-war prosperity. To the new cultured class the severe doctrines of their forebears, even when not openly denied were being quietly dropped. This fact was brought strikingly to Morse's attention one day while he was in a Boston bookstore. By chance he picked up a little tract called "Divine and Moral Songs; revised and altered, so as to render them of general use . . ." and noticed that the doctrines of the Divinity of Christ, etc., were omitted from this revision. Consequently he wrote an article entitled "Beware of Counterfeits," in which he declared that "if this should pass upon the public unnoticed, from altering children's books, more important alterations might be undertaken, until, grown bold in the business, even the sacred truths of the Holy Bible may be in danger." [28] The article was published in the Boston *Columbian Centinel*, and was signed "A Friend of Honesty."

Morse had received his training in a section where the influence of wealth and trade had not yet permeated. Now, in the face of this alien sentiment he clung desperately to the orthodox doctrines of his New England religion, tempered as they were by the logical demands of the New Divinity. His religious temperament was already firmly set. He was convinced of his duty, and interpreted his life mission in terms of being a loyal "ambassador of Christ" in an age of

[28] See W. B. Sprague, *Life of Morse*, pp. 54, 55.

indifference and disintegration. The complacent resented this energetic enthusiast largely because his methods aroused what they believed to be unchristian emotions and led to a bigoted spirit of partisanship. Even Bentley felt that the manner of Freeman's attack on Morse's *Geography* was unfortunate. "All love to see pride debased," he said, "but confess the Taste difficult to ingenuous virtue." [29]

Morse apparently showed marked ability in handling controversial questions. When Green visited Charlestown, he wrote that he "spent the morning with Mr. Morse who read me his controversies from the pulpit and the press with the anti-Trinitarians and the Baptists. He writes with a closeness and correctness, and an aptitude for controversy which exceeds the expectation (which was not low) that I had formed of his talents." [30]

One gathers from this remark that the Presbyterians, of whom Green was one, had hoped that Morse would be a strong defender of evangelical religion in the Boston area. Morse was encouraged by Green's visit. Wrote Green again,

I feel myself strongly attached to this worthy man; and he says that my coming has served to encourage him and strengthen him in his sentiments and preaching. He is opposed to the prevailing opinions of Arianism and Arminianism, and to indifference in religion. Yet he acts with suitable meekness, and what I think is a true Christian spirit, that is, he is firm and fervent, and yet not bitter or censorious. He appears to be a man of great humility, of a warm heart, a great understanding, and considerable improvement.[31]

Morse was instrumental in having his friend and classmate Abiel Holmes settle in a church near him at Cambridge in the hope that Holmes would strengthen the cause of evangelical religion. Several days before the installation service,

[29] Bentley, *Diary*, II, 70.
[30] J. H. Jones: *Life of Ashbel Green*, p. 224.
[31] *Ibid.*, p. 218.

Lieutenant Governor Samuel Phillips wrote thus to Morse concerning the candidate: "From the character I have had of the Rev. gentleman [Mr. Holmes] who is about to take the particular charge of the First Church and congregation at Cambridge, I feel, as a member of the great Christian family, much indebted to you, sir, for the influence I am led to believe you had in bringing about the event. I hope for important good consequences therefrom to the university, and through that to many of our churches, as well as to that church in particular." [32]

Morse and Holmes, with essentially the same background and training, were in agreement theologically. Payson Williston recalled his classmate Holmes: "He always . . . held to the orthodox faith. He was cautious, some might say even to a fault; though there were some cases in which he acted with great decision." [33] Dr. Jenks also indicated that Morse might find an ally in his friend at Cambridge. "Dr. Holmes," he wrote, "was eminently of the conservative class, not of the revolutionary. He loved religion cordially; but the religion he loved was not denunciation, censorious or canting . . . it was rational, obedient, reverential and resigned to God 'full of mercy and good fruits, without partiality and without hypocrisy' . . . the Hopkinsian portion of our Divines could not claim him, nor could the Arminian class. He believed in the necessity of a radical change of the affections to constitute the religious character, and that this change was wrought by the Holy Spirit; and the Divinity of the Saviour he expressly maintained." [34]

Holmes's settlement at Cambridge aroused the same unanimity of feeling and satisfaction as had Morse's at Charles-

[32] Sprague, *Life of Morse*, p. 26.
[33] Sprague, *Annals of the American Pulpit*, II, 244.
[34] *Ibid.*, p. 246.

town. The learned dignity and literary ability of the new pastor impressed a congregation so close to Harvard. Stiles says that the Honorable Colonel Nathaniel Gorham of Charlestown claims that "they are all pleased with Mr. Holmes both at Cambridge and round about Boston and elsewhere." [35] President Willard wrote on January 26, 1792, with evident satisfaction, that Holmes "is free from that self-sufficiency and positiveness, which some young men are full of, which is disgusting to all around and is a great bar to their own advancement in valuable knowledge." [36]

Shortly after this event David Tappan, pastor of the church in Newbury, was elected professor of theology at Harvard College. Morse was acquainted with Tappan and knew him to be a strong ally of evangelical truth. Consequently, as a member of the Board of Overseers of the College he had used his influence to secure Tappan, and by his contacts with several of the wealthy members of his own parish was successful in raising the amount asked by the Newbury church for Tappan's release.[37]

As the century drew to a close Morse threw himself more and more into activities for promoting evangelical religion. Through his stimulation of the question of Baptism, the Concert of Prayer (in coöperation with the Presbyterians), as well as through his lectures and articles, he sought to arouse the people of New England from their indifference. At times he was to feel the loneliness of his chosen mission and a sense of being at odds with his liberal environment. In a letter on Feb. 7, 1791, he wrote that he stood "solitary among my brethren in the public defense of this doctrine [the Trinity]." [38] His religious sentiments were contrary to the grow-

[35] Ezra Stiles, *Diary*, III, 439.
[36] I. M. Calder, ed. *Letters and Papers of Ezra Stiles*, 1933, p. 117.
[37] Sprague, *Life of Morse*, pp. 26–27.
[38] *Ibid.*, p. 52.

49

ing latitudinarian atmosphere of the Boston area so that practically every move he made precipitated opposition. Otherwise he might well have fitted into the general spirit of the section. Morse might have swelled the rising tide of Unitarianism had he gone to Harvard or had he been reared at Salem. But his whole thought was founded upon the new orthodoxy that prevailed further south and that raised him as a petulant champion against the intellectual and religious fashions of Boston.

CHAPTER V

MORSE AND THE ILLUMINATI

MORSE's first outstanding controversy [1] came toward the close of the century. Until this time he had been content with decrying the lack of religious fervor and trying to strengthen the forces of evangelical religion wherever he could. But events conspired about 1798 to urge him to carry the battle aggressively into the enemy's territory. In common with the majority of his ministerial friends, he believed the current assumption that one of the strongest sources of irreligion in this country was the French school of thought. During a visit to his Alma Mater at New Haven he noticed the lack of religious enthusiasm and the bold nicknames by which the students addressed one another. Beecher remembered that "most of the class . . . called each other Voltaire, Rousseau, D'Alembert, etc." [2]

In January, Morse wrote to Dr. Erskine of Edinburgh, "the French treat us shamefully, and seem determined either to subject us to their influence and control,—which they never can do,—or to plunge us into war. They have a busy, intriguing and unprincipled party among us, which, though numerous, is, I hope, diminishing." [3] This reflected Morse's

---

[1] This incident in Morse's career has been treated so thoroughly by Vernon Stauffer in his *New England and the Bavarian Illuminati* that the following few pages are little more than a summary of his account, and are included merely to complete the narrative, and to give the larger setting of this particular controversy.

[2] Lyman Beecher, *Autobiography and Correspondence of Lyman Beecher,* edited by Charles Beecher, p. 43.

[3] W. B. Sprague, *Life of Jedidiah Morse,* p. 231.

Federalist sympathies and his concurrence in the belief that the French minister and agents were in secret league with influential representatives of the Democratic party.[4] It was natural for the defenders of Massachusetts' sacred institutions to jump at any definite explanation which promised a simple and speedy solution of their increasingly precarious position. This French influence seemed a point at which the enemy of revealed religion appeared clear-cut and definite. Here was a factor which could be investigated and attacked. The evangelical clergy were not long in taking advantage of this opportunity. Set afloat in the stormy sea of a new nation and society, many intelligent and sincere men of piety grasped at the nearest straw. Though there was some foundation of truth for the accusation, still the more indigenous causes of irreligion were difficult to combat and escaped attention.

One would expect Morse to be a leader in this attack. His many friends were neither silent nor inactive. Less than a year after Morse had been instrumental in settling David Tappan as Professor of Divinity at Harvard College, the Professor preached in Morse's pulpit bemoaning the corrupted state of religion, "due to the bold advance and rapid diffusion of 'sceptical, deistical, and other loose and pernicious sentiments.' " Growing more confident, he continued, "May I not add that a species of atheistical philosophy, which has of late triumphantly reared its head in Europe, and which affects to be the offspring and nurse of sound reason, science and liberty, seems in danger of infecting some of the more sprightly and free-thinking geniuses of America." [5]

Likewise, his good friend David Osgood, who gave him the right hand of Fellowship at the Installation Council, a

---

[4] See Stauffer, *New England and the Bavarian Illuminati*, p. 128.
[5] *Ibid.*, pp. 88–89.

year later was heard adding his voice to the gathering spirit of fear. He delivered a

vehement denunciation of the Democratic Societies, because of their subservience to foreign emissaries, and because of the outrageous activities of Minister Genet. Not content with this, he proceeded to lay heavy emphasis upon the ferocious zeal and desperate fury which the French were manifesting in their attacks upon the institutions of religion, the far-reaching import of which, he declared, was already apparent in the fact that, under the power of their blind devotion to the French cause, not a few American citizens were casting off their allegiance to the Christian religion.[6]

Joseph Lathrop of West Springfield, a sympathetic friend of Morse, also entered the fray with a sermon entitled "God's Challenge to Infidels to Defend Their Cause. . . ."

Nor was this attitude limited to Morse's section of New England. A Connecticut preacher, Nathan Strong, of the North Presbyterian Church in Hartford, preached similar sentiments on the occasion of the State Fast in 1798. The General Assembly of the Presbyterian Church in the United States, meeting in Philadelphia, made the following statement:

When formidable innovations and convulsions in Europe threaten destruction to morals and religion; when scenes of devastation and bloodshed, unexampled in the history of modern nations, have convulsed the world; and when our own country is threatened with similar calamities; insensibility in us would be stupidity; silence would be criminal. The watchmen on Zion's walls are bound by their commission to sound a general alarm at the approach of danger. We therefore desire to direct your awakened attention, towards that bursting stream, which threatens to sweep before it the religious principles, institutions, and morals of our people. We are filled with a deep concern and an awful dread, whilst we announce it as our real conviction, that the eternal God has a controversy with our nation, and is

[6] *Ibid.*, p. 90.

53

about to visit us in his sore displeasure. A solemn crisis has arrived, in which we are called to the most serious contemplation of the moral causes which have produced it, and the measures which it becomes us to pursue.[7]

The New Divinity leader and President of Yale, Timothy Dwight, was noted for his attacks upon all evidences of infidelity and irreligion. "It is safe to say that among all the men in New England no man's spirit was more persistently haunted by the fear that the forces of irreligion were in league to work general ruin to the institutions of society than his."[8] On September 9, 1797, he gave two discourses on the "Nature and Danger of Infidel Philosophy," to the graduating students of the college. On the last page of his printed discourses is the following note:

Since these discourses were sent to the press, I have seen a work lately published in Great Britain, and republished in America, written by J. Robison, Prof. of Natural Philosophy in the University of Edinburgh, and Secretary of the Royal Society in that city, and entitled, "A Conspiracy against All the Governments and Religions in Europe." In this work the reader may see the dangers of Infidel Philosophy set in the strongest light possible. He may see a plan formed, and to an alarming degree executed, for exterminating Christianity, Natural Religion, the belief of a God, of the immortality of the Soul, and Moral Obligation; for rooting out of the world civil and domestic government, the right of property, marriage, natural affection, chastity, and decency; and in a word for destroying whatever is virtuous, refined or desirable, and introducing again savageness and brutism. . . .[9]

The first person to call Morse's attention to an organized effort in Europe to overthrow religion was his friend Dr.

[7] *Acts and Proceedings of the General Assembly* . . . May 17, 1798, cited *ibid.*, p. 100.
[8] *Ibid.*, p. 246. See also G. A. Koch. *Republican Religion*, pp. 254–57.
[9] Timothy Dwight, "Sermon on the Nature and Danger of Infidel Philosophy," Sept. 9, 1779, p. 95.

Erskine of Edinburgh. He wrote to Morse in January, 1797, telling him that people were alarmed in Europe over a conspiracy and mentioned Robison's volume which was about to be published. But Morse did not see a copy until the following year. An article in the *Independent Chronicle*, January 14, 1798, told how he happened to secure one.

The first copies which were sent to America, arrived at Philadelphia and New York, at both which places the re-printing of it was immediately undertaken, and the Philadelphia edition was completed ready for sale in the short space of three weeks. This was about the middle of April. Happening at this time to be in Philadelphia and hearing the work spoken of in terms of the highest respect by men of judgment, one of them went so far as to pronounce it the most interesting work that the present century had produced; I was induced to procure a copy, which I brought home with me. . . .[10]

With this copy burning in his hand and mind, Morse waited less than a month to explode the news of the danger to the public. President Adams's Fast Day proclamation offered the occasion and set the stage. The United States was " 'at present placed in a hazardous and afflictive position.' The necessity of sounding a loud call to repentance and reformation was declared to be imperative, and the people were fervently urged to implore Heaven's mercy and benediction on the imperiled nation." [11] Consequently, on May 9, 1798, Morse delivered his memorable Fast Day Sermon to the people of the North Church in Boston and to his own congregation in Charlestown. He warned the people of the United States that the secret European association of Illuminati was actively scheming to overthrow their civil and religious institutions.[12] No doubt Morse was sincere in introducing this matter: "I hold it a duty," he declared, "which I owe to God, to

---

[10] Stauffer, *New England and the Bavarian Illuminati*, p. 233, note.
[11] *Ibid.*, p. 229.
[12] *Ibid.*, p. 11.

the cause of religion, to my country, and to you, at this time, to declare to you, thus honestly and faithfully, these truths. My only aim is to awaken in you and myself a due attention, at this alarming period, to our dearest interests. As a faithful watchman I would give you warning of your present danger." [13]

This sermon would not have involved any extraordinary consequences, since it was habitual with the clergy of that period to use such national occasions for their political exhortations. But, it was the element of Illuminism which gave peculiar significance to Morse's utterance.[14] Whether he did it intentionally or not, Morse furnished evangelical religion with a shibboleth by which it could fight its battle against the growing spirit of irreligion.[15] It was natural for Morse, driven by his intense desire to save religion, and firmly convinced of the truth of his evangelistic sentiments, to exaggerate his claim, even beyond all factual evidence. He and his friends utilized this opportunity to its fullest measure—draining its possibilities to the last drop.

Opponents soon lifted a protesting voice. In the battle of correspondence and newspaper articles Morse was unsparingly attacked. "I am informed," wrote a friend to the liberal Salem pastor, "that the author of that illebial [illiberal] and malevolent piece against me is *Morse*. I wish to know for a certainty before I take notice of it. I will ask him if I cannot find it out any other way. It resembles his manner. I will treat him with less respect than his opponents have done. I will tell him what mischief his erroneous and exaggerated account of America has done in Britain, and also expose *his ignorance in other things*. If Morse be the author he is a liar,

---

[13] Jedidiah Morse, *Sermon on the National Fast*, May 9, 1798, p. 25.
[14] See Stauffer, *op. cit.*, p. 238.
[15] *Ibid.*, p. 239.

for he knows my political opinion." [16] There was adequate proof to substantiate this accusation of Morse. Most of the sources of his proofs of the Illuminism conspiracy were fed to him by his Federalist friends, particularly Oliver Wolcott.[17] In spite of an apparent sincerity in raising the whole issue, believing that it would strengthen the cause of religion, he was soon engulfed in the political implications far beyond his depth. He wrote that he was persuaded "you will properly appreciate my motives in making the above communication, as also in publishing the Sermon and Appendix. I live among a people many of whom err in Sentiment and Conduct through their want of information. It was especially for their benefit that the Appendix was compiled." [18]

Though it is well to keep in mind the political motivation of this controversy as it has been made clear by Stauffer, we wish here merely to call attention to the more strictly religious and ecclesiastical aspects. Dwight, Morse, and their fellows, when they discovered that they as "moderates" held a middle ground, did their utmost to gain religious leadership away from both right and left (Old and New Lights vs. Unitarians and Liberals). The method employed was this attempt to unite all religious groups, in spite of their growing rivalry, in a common cause against a very dangerous common enemy.

Dwight's efforts in Connecticut were meeting with success and Morse was anxious to serve the cause in his Boston environment. Little had he foreseen the vociferous attack which resulted from his exposure of the Illuminati conspiracy and the personal abuse and embarrassment which he was forced to endure. On November 30, 1799, he wrote to his father:

[16] F. Nichols, Letter to W. Bentley; Jan. 28, 1799, in the Essex Institute, Salem, Vol. I, No. 56.
[17] See Stauffer, p. 300, note 2.
[18] Ibid., p. 270.

You may probably have heard how abusively I have been treated in Babcock's paper of Hartford in regard to a letter I received from Prof. Ebeling of Hamburg. . . . I can only say that Samuel Huntington of Norwich, member of Assembly, was at my house last July and heard a part of the letter—and has had the meaness and wickedness to fabricate and propagate the vilest calumnies against Prof. Robison, and to palm them on this letter—and through him it has got into the Hartford paper with some low and scurrilous abuse of me, prefixed and annexed. . . . Huntington, I am informed, is a Jacobin and a Mason— If their principles lead to, or countenance such conduct, they ought to be detested by every friend to social happiness. . . . The issue I do not fear, but it is troublesome defending one's self against such vile attacks. The circumstances attending this attack are extremely aggravating.[19]

The long and heated controversy ended only when Morse was unable to substantiate the proofs of his claim.[20] It is sufficient to say that it resulted in a stimulation of both parties —the defenders and interpreters of orthodoxy, and the liberal group which held Unitarian sentiments. Every New Divinity preacher of any concern was drawn in on the side of the Calvinists,[21] while the more broad-minded of the clergy became conscious of their differing attitudes. The future trend of the conflict between these parties was more clearly defined because of this emotional outburst. When the smoke had cleared away, Morse saw that the gains had been meager, and realized that he must turn to more organized and positive attempts to revive and strengthen evangelical religion.

[19] Yale Letter, Nov. 30, 1799.
[20] See Stauffer, pp. 320, 321.
[21] Ibid., pp. 272–75, 309.

CHAPTER VI

PROPAGANDA FOR PRESBYTERIANISM

MORSE immediately employed two methods to accomplish his purpose of uniting the orthodox: one, strengthening ministerial fellowship in some form of ecclesiastical association; and second, editing periodicals by means of which the mass of people could be influenced and stimulated in evangelical sentiments.

We have already noted his sympathy with the Presbyterians on numerous occasions. There is evidence that he was extremely anxious to establish a similar form of ecclesiastical organization in his section of New England in order to support his work and to stem the tide of error. He envied his Connecticut colleagues and their Presbyterian Consociations by which they obtained their ends. Yale college under Dwight's stimulation was experiencing a revival of interest in evangelical religion and Morse longed to create such a reaction at Charlestown and his vicinity. Consequently he bent his efforts toward establishing a closer relationship between the Congregationalists of his state and the Presbyterians to the south of him.

In the course of Dr. Green's visit with Morse in 1791, the affinity of their opinions no doubt led to a discussion of the possibility of such a coöperation. Green had indicated his lack of any hope for unity in the Boston Association [1] and agreed with Morse that some form of working relationship with the Presbyterians was quite desirable. In a letter to Green dated

---

[1] See p. 36, above.

September 1, 1792, Morse revealed his own sentiments and those of his Boston environment in the matter:

Till the cause of "liberality" is revived among you (referring to an unsuccessful attempt that had just been made in Philadelphia to establish a Unitarian preacher), or we become illiberal like you, I doubt if a friendly intercourse can be established between Presbyterians and Congregationalists, as some of us "narrow folks" strive for. Mr. Eckley informs me he has written you on the subject. He is one of a Committee with myself and others to report a Plan of friendly correspondence with our Presbyterian brethren. But we shall effect nothing. Too many will throw cold water on every thing of the kind. With the utmost difficulty a few of us got a Committee appointed to deliberate on the subject and report our opinions. The Committee compose half almost of all the friends of the measure. If all our plans are frustrated, I apprehend the aggrieved party will think seriously of forming themselves into a separate Body, and framing an ecclesiastical constitution for themselves, and one too which will admit of such an intercourse with the Presbyterian Church, as will be mutually agreeable and beneficial. But this is sub rosa for the present.[2]

The result of this attempt was as Morse predicted. A form of friendly correspondence and weak coöperation was established between the General Assembly of the Presbyterian Church, the General Association of Connecticut, and the Massachusetts Convention of ministers, particularly on the point of recognizing candidates bearing credentials from these groups. The Presbyterians were frankly enthusiastic about the possibility of strengthening religion but sceptical about the influence which might be brought to bear upon their group. "I hope the union will promote the interests of religion, as well as a more extensive intercourse between the ministers of your churches and ours," wrote Green to Morse, "but be careful you do not send us men of 'liberal' sentiments, for our churches will not endure them." [3] "I cannot

[2] W. B. Sprague, *Life of Jedidiah Morse*, pp. 73, 74.
[3] *Ibid.*, p. 75.

but flatter myself that the intercourse now opened between the General Assembly and our Convention . . . will issue in great good to our churches and to the cause of religion," [4] Morse wrote back optimistically.

Though hope burned steadfastly in this man's heart, his dream of intimate coöperation was not destined to be realized. Opposition came from various quarters. The liberals of Unitarian sentiments were largely indifferent to it or disinclined to encourage it, while positive obstruction appeared in the New Lights, and particularly the influential Dr. Emmons of Franklin. His memorable dictum was, "Associationism leads to Consociationism; Consociationism to Presbyterianism; Presbyterianism leads to Episcopacy; Episcopacy leads to Roman Catholicism; and Roman Catholicism is an ultimate fact." [5]

This attitude was expressed again and again by Emmons. On another occasion he wrote:

Congregationalists often complain of Presbyterians, Episcopalians and Papists, on account of their church government: but they have no reason to complain, for they act upon precisely the same principles, when they concentrate and increase their ecclesiastical power by union with associations, consociations, and ecclesiastical councils. When any church gives up its independence to any other ecclesiastical body, it gives up all its power. But Christ has given no power to churches which they may give away. Congregational churches at this day ought to be on their guard, and strenuously maintain their independence. [6]

The Hopkinsians as a group were particularly wary of Morse's attempts to draw them into coöperation with the Presbyterians. Each attempt to introduce the principles of Consociationism was crushed by the influence of Emmons and Spring, who used as their watchword: "Beware of the Con-

[4] W. B. Sprague, *Life of Jedidiah Morse*, p. 75.
[5] E. A. Park, *Memoir of Nathanael Emmons*, p. 163.
[6] *Ibid.*, note on pp. 163–64.

cision." Emmons believed that there was a danger that Presbyterian tendencies would be carried from the churches into the Commonwealth.[7]

Faced with this cautious opposition from the Hopkinsians, and having to overcome the conspicuous indifference on the part of the liberals, Morse turned his energies from coöperation with the Presbyterians to a more direct attempt to unify the orthodox ministers of Massachusetts. The Illuminati scare was producing an emotional stimulus which could well be utilized for this purpose. Consequently, Morse formulated the following letter, had it published, and circularized among the ministers of the state:

Deeply impressed ourselves with the critical and very alarming state of our country and of our holy Religion . . . permit us affectionately to invite you to join with us in taking serious and prayerful consideration of the unusual increase of infidelity and impiety among us. . . . Are not the following among other vices, too generally prevalent among us, viz. disregard and even contempt of the sabbath and other religious ordinances, profaneness, variance, emulations, strife, sedition, heresies, envyings, evil speaking, intemperance, impiety, unfaithfulness, dishonesty, and an inordinate love and pursuit of wealth? Is it not true that . . . vital religion, among real Christians is decaying, and a spirit of indifference prevailing?[8]

He urged in this letter that some system to combat this indifference be devised, suggesting that each association send one or more delegates to meet at Boston before the annual elections in May "to consult on the general interests of religion, and the means conducive to its support and advancement."

This appeal aroused the friends of Morse and they responded with their encouragement. It is significant that the

[7] *Ibid.*, p. 165.
[8] Letter owned by the Connecticut Historical Society, April 15, 1799.

strongest support for coöperation came from the western portion of New England.[9] The "genteel" ease and religious indifference of the seaboard communities, caused largely by the rapid acquisition of wealth and by contact with European thought, had not, as yet, permeated this section. Life on the frontier was isolated in small communities, remote from the main currents of the world's life, and was particularly devoid of the emotional satisfactions of the coastal cities. The inhabitants of Boston and the mercantile centers found emotional expression in their commercial and other activities. But the people of the western, agricultural section had no such outlet. In consequence, they evidenced a warmer response to religion and, particularly, an enthusiasm for its evangelical and revivalistic aspects. The success in this section of the Methodists and Baptists, with their emotional emphasis, further illustrates the point. Robert C. Miller, in his "Historical Discourse on the 50th Anniversary of the Formation of the First Baptist Church of Salem," remarked that "at the commencement of this century, revivals of religion of a marked character were enjoyed in the Congregational churches of the extreme western part of this state, and the contiguous north-western portions of Conn. The ministers whose congregations were thus blessed were Timothy Cooley, Samuel Shepard, Jeremiah Hallock, Edward D. Griffin and Ebenezer Porter. Not so favored was this portion of the State, filled as too many pulpits were, with men who held other views than these did of the Gospel and the way of life."[10]

Joseph Buckminster, who had been a student at Yale with

[9] Ministers in many of the frontier sections, particularly in Berkshire County, were overwhelmingly Yale men.

[10] Discourse by Robert C. Miller, on the 50th Anniversary of First Baptist Church, Salem, Mass., p. 12.

Dwight and was his personal friend,[11] wrote to Morse from his parish at Portsmouth, New Hampshire:

I am pleased to see the ministers of Boston awakened to a sense of the dangers which beset our altars and shrines. While I am sorry for the foreign accession to the flood of error and infidelity, which has been long swelling in this country, it appears to me that a departure from pure evangelical principles, and a silence respecting the peculiarly humbling, awakening and affecting doctrines of the Gospel in the public teachers of it, have contributed their full share to the evil. I am in no apprehension that you are included in this charge. I have heard and seen of your firmness and steadfastness in the truth. But is it not too true that ministers in general, and especially our younger ministers, leave the humiliating state of man as an apostate creature, his helplessness and danger, the glorious character of Christ as a Divine person, the special influences of the Spirit, the necessity of regeneration, and the awful prospects of the impenitent and unbelieving, out of their public discourses; which they fill with philosophical or moral essays and popular harangues. . . . But is there nothing to be done by us? . . . Might not Association meetings be so improved? After this, we might, with greater confidence and hope of success, have more seasons of public prayer, following our devotions with a fervent spirit of Divine things in all our converse with the world.[12]

Buckminster undoubtedly felt a real need for Association meetings which would provide the revivalists with the means of strengthening one another in their work, and expressed his utmost confidence in the efforts Morse was making.

Mr. Nash, Moderator of the Hampshire Association of ministers, communicated his concern to the Charlestown pastor on October 21, 1799: "Sectaries and Schismatics and illiterate (Itinerants) we also have had with us, and we have found the best way not to oppose them but to treat them with kindness when their sentiments and conduct would authorize it,—and with silent neglect in other cases to endeavor

[11] See Sprague, *Annals*, II, 109.
[12] W. B. Sprague, *Life of Jedidiah Morse*, pp. 76–77.

to counteract their influence by a more diligent and zealous attention to our ministerial duties." [13]

In spite of this encouragement, Morse and his friends despaired of accomplishing their purpose through the Convention of Massachusetts Ministers, so they proceeded to form a separate body on the basis of their common belief. On July 7, 1802, eight district associations were represented at a meeting in Northampton, at which the General Association was formed. The Assembly's Shorter Catechism was made the basis of their union and fellowship. Later in a letter to Dr. Lathrop, Morse explained the object of this group:

It was intended merely to awaken attention to, and to revive the Christian spirit, energy, and faithfulness in church discipline and government of former times, "to strengthen the things that remain and are ready to die." . . . My desire is that our churches may be brought back to the old paths and good ways of the Fathers of New England, with such modification and improvement as may be consonant with the Scriptures, and adapted to the present state of society and of the times. . . . I have long thought that something like the measure contemplated was indispensable to the preservation of our Congregational Churches. If we proceed ten years longer in our present loose, desultory, diverse and contentious manner of conducting our ecclesiastical government and discipline, the various sectaries . . . will well nigh root out our denomination. The State laws already favour them, and probably will do so more and more. I see no way so likely to preserve the things which remain, and which are thus threatened, as a General Association to confer and act together upon the great concerns of our churches; and perhaps, should it be thought best, to revive, revise and re-establish our Cambridge Platform. [14]

Though the General Association united those of "liberal-orthodox" sentiments, still Morse was not satisfied with its limitations and tried to broaden the basis of coöperation. He wrote to his friend, Dr. Lyman of Hatfield, urging him to

[13] Yale Letter, Oct. 21, 1799.
[14] Sprague, *Life of Jedidiah Morse*, pp. 85–87.

bring up the question of the State ecclesiastical constitution at the coming Convention of Massachusetts Ministers. "If we can preserve union and avoid disunion, by some concessions and sacrifices, it will be best. And I hope that, with due care and exertions, this may be done." [15] Lyman replied that he thought "Moderate Presbyterianism is the Scripture Platform. . . . We must all be Christians upon the doctrines of grace, or we may as well not call ourselves Christians at all. And a belief of these doctrines being first had, great indulgence is to be given to all other differences of opinion." [16]

To Morse the situation was intense. "The Ruler of the Universe," he wrote, "appears to be preparing us and other parts of Christendom for trying conflicts. The world is peculiarly convulsed and will not I believe be calmed till it shall have been purified as by fire." [17] He further conveyed his alarm to Lyman on the 15th of November:

The subject of "Platform or Ecclesiastical Constitution" is reviving here and must be brought to a point next May or the Congregational interest will be split to pieces—to the great injury of religion, and the rejoicing of sectaries. We must unite on some middle ground. I wish you to put pen to paper on the subject and shew forcibly the necessity of some bond of Union and general rule of church government—the importance of union and point out the best means of accomplishing these things. Somebody must write and publish. All likeminded must have an understanding with each other and act in concert. The two extremes (the Arminians and Hopkinsians) must be conciliated or else strength enough be collected on the middle ground (that is the ground occupied by the Old Calvinists and the Moderate Calvinists) to do without them. I believe the thing can be accomplished, if undertaken with resolution and pursued with a Christian spirit.[18]

[15] *Ibid.*, p. 78.
[16] *Ibid.*, p. 79.
[17] Yale Letter, October 11, 1803.
[18] Yale Letter, Nov. 15, 1803; also part in Sprague, *Life of Jedidiah Morse*, p. 79.

Throughout this period, Morse was extremely busy. Dr. Osgood of Medford wrote that

a few weeks preceding the late Convention of Congregational ministers at Boston, my good neighbor the Rev. Dr. Morse, proposed to me
as a matter which a number of our brethren were desirous of having
brought forward at said convention, the choosing of a committee to
revise our platform, that there might be more order and uniformity in
our church affairs. I asked, in reply, "Have you not read my Dudleian
Sermon? Yes!" At the Convention Morse whispered in my ear, "Will
you be one of the committee? The committee for what? Why you
know what I mentioned to you some time since about revising the
platform. Brother Morse, if you bring forward that business, I will
grind you to powder!" . . . He is, for the most part, wonderfully
busy on those occasions, always devising what he considers as good
things.[19]

Fear of opposition led Morse to lay cautious plans. "There
will be much to fear from the opposers of Christ's Divinity,"
wrote Lyman, "and perhaps no less from some of our Hopkinsian brethren, who are high Independents. If anybody can
coalesce the contending parties upon a safe and promising
basis, it will be happy. Who can do more than my friend
Morse?" [20]

Consequently, when the subject came before the Convention on May 30, 1804, a committee, with President Willard
of Harvard as chairman, was appointed to inquire by letter
of the several district Associations concerning their opinion of
the plan of a General Association, and the further possibility of coöperation. Those who replied favorably were again
largely the western groups: Berkshire, Brookfield, Hampshire Central, Hampshire North, Haverhill, Mountain, and
Westford. A few of the Associations were undecided: Plymouth, Salem (declined to express an opinion, but sent a del-

[19] *Monthly Religious Magazine*, XXXI (Feb., 1864), 97.
[20] Sprague, *Life of Jedidiah Morse*, p. 80.

egate to get information), Barnstable (in favor of some union but objected to forcing creed or confession), Unity (desired some modification in the proposed plan). The group opposed were: Essex, Middle, Marlboro', Worcester. Boston dissented in a "kind and courteous spirit," which was expressed in a paper stating that the city approved "the sentiments in which the proposal appears to have originated [those of friendly cooperation]," but that

considering the state of religious opinion, and the spirit and circumstances of the time, we are led to believe that no practicable plan of this nature can be formed and we are apprehensive that the proposed measure for promoting harmony will be more likely to interrupt it . . . tending, it argues by discussions upon doctrinal bases, to "an erection of barriers between those who at present are not formally separated, and the bonds of union would be strengthened between those only who are already sufficiently cemented." It insists equally strongly that usefulness will be impaired, rather than assisted, particularly by the tendency to uphold "human standards of opinion" which might be so active in erecting prejudice against dissentients as to exhibit a "spirit of uncharitableness and censoriousness produced, and the teachers of religion placed under powerful temptations either to shun declaring the whole counsel of God, or to teach for doctrines the commandments of men." [21]

Before the committee could make its report at the Convention, the death of Chairman Willard dealt, according to Morse, "a serious blow to the object." Morse added, "Dr. Forbes, another member of the Committee, friendly to the plan, is sick probably unto death. Nil desperandum, however, is my motto. Let us faithfully do our duty and leave the event. Great pains are taken to defeat the object. . . ." [22]

[21] A. H. Quint, Article in *Congregationalist*, Nov. 27, 1857. (Note: The references are made to Dr. J. Clark's articles in the *Congregationalist* on the Ecclesiastical History of Massachusetts.)

[22] Sprague, *Life of Jedidiah Morse*, letter to Dr. Joseph Lyman, Dec. 4, 1805, p. 81.

In case the committee's report was not accepted by the ministers, Morse advised that some plan of uniting those who were in agreement be held ready: "something to rally around in case of defeat." [23] "You must be armed in complete panoply," he advised Lyman, "for you will be placed in the forefront of the hottest battle." [24] And he added later, "Much will depend on you and the gentlemen from your quarter." [25]

In spite of all these careful preparations on the part of Morse and his friends, opposition to the report of the committee suggesting coöperation was so strong that no vote was taken and the measure failed. Nathanael Emmons, the outstanding Hopkinsian, preached the Convention sermon in which he stated that

Unity of faith is the only proper basis of unity of spirit. Christians may be and must be united in affection, so far as they are united in sentiment: but so far as they are disunited in sentiment, they are and must be disunited in affection. There is, therefore, no propriety, nor prospect of success, in attempting to unite the professed friends of Christ in brotherly love, without first uniting them in the belief of the same essential doctrines of the gospel.

But supposing, that the whole Christian world could be brought to unite in affection, while they retain all their different and inconsistent opinions, it would be utterly wrong to attempt it. For, if Christians should form such a coalition, it would be criminal in itself, and highly injurious to the cause of religion. They would disobey the divine injunction, "to be perfectly joined together in the same mind and in the same judgment." They would become an unchristian combination, to countenance and support each other in all their errors and delusions of Deists, Atheists, and Sceptics. And they would actually exercise that same kind of catholicism, which heretics and infidels have so long been pleading for, and by which they have done more mischief to Christianity, than by any other weapon, which they have ever employed against it. Under the pretext of promoting universal toleration, they

[23] Yale Letter, May 2, 1805.
[24] Sprague, *Life of Jedidiah Morse*, p. 81.
[25] Yale Letter, May 2, 1805.

have taught multitudes and multitudes, to extend their catholicism to disbelievers, deniers, and opposers of the gospel. This unlimited catholicism naturally tends to subvert the gospel, and to involve the whole world in error and infidelity. Let none, therefore, cherish this spirit, and strengthen the hearts and hands of the enemies of truth, by attempting to unite Christians in affection, without uniting them in the belief of the great and essential doctrines of Christianity.[26]

Emmons further stated his opposition to the plan in a later letter to Lyman:

Though you and I call ourselves Calvinists, and that justly, yet there are very visible shades of difference in our religious opinions. In your body, there is a large number of my sentiments and a larger number of yours. . . . Your side will beyond all doubt, carry their points. This would be the case, were there only two parties in the Association. There are more than two; there may be ten. There are some old Calvinists, some Hopkinsians, some semi-Calvinists and semi-Arminians, some Congregationalists, and many Presbyterians. These last, in respect to numbers, reputation, and talents, are superior to all the other members of the union. . . . Undoubtedly, the Presbyterians will be the center . . . those of your cast will naturally unite with them in points of discipline; those of my cast must make greater sacrifices and give up their peculiar sentiments, in regard both to doctrine and discipline to the Presbyterians. The Semi-Calvinists and Semi-Arminians must come up or down, which you please, to the Calvinist and Presbyterian standard. The final result will be a general union according to the immutable laws of Presbyterians.[27]

The liberal Bentley of Salem expressed the opposition of his group by a comment in his diary:

Was [at the] convention of the Congregational Clergy. Dr. Emmons preached. By his metaphysical subtlety, he endeavored to persuade us that there really was one mind among Christians, that the means of attaining were simple, and that we had a right and indeed a necessity of denying all who differed from us our affections. The most illiberal

[26] Nathanael Emmons: *A Sermon Preached before the Convention of the Congregational Ministers in Boston*, May 31, 1804.
[27] E. A. Park, *Memoirs of Emmons*, p. 170.

discourse I ever heard. As soon as sermon was over, the Convention opened by adjournment. The business I did not know till this stage of it. It seems Morse and Co. had contemplated a Union, a Consocation of Churches as I might call it. To fix it a committee from the 21 associations was intended who could report some plan. Superior men such as Dr. Osgood, Cummings, etc. saw the difficulty and the evil and that the plan could not succeed and must excite alarm. After all that was said of one mind we divided 35 and 35 and finally one in the negative gave us our wishes. Then a committee of 9 persons were chosen to write to the associations, to meet before Convention, and report and so we trust we have gotten rid of this business which was designed to betray the clergy into the hands of some evil and artful enthusiasts. As the plan was not fully developed, we must judge the well-known characters of men who enter into such designs.[28]

This defeat of his plans did not discourage Morse. "I hope," he wrote to Lyman, "all evangelical men will cordially unite their influence and efforts. I consider Unitarianism, as the democracy of Christianity. It dissolves all the bonds of Christian union, and deprives religion of all its efficacy and influence upon society. Our ecclesiastical affairs are fast assuming the portentous aspect and confused state of our political affairs. It becomes us to be clothed with the whole armour of God and to be ready for the conflict." [29]

Time and time again through the ensuing years, the Charlestown pastor made vigorous efforts to broaden the power and influence of the orthodox General Association. Appealing to Dr. Lathrop in 1808, he wrote,

If gentlemen of your age and standing and influence in the churches could feel willing to co-operate in conducting a General Association, I am persuaded all would go harmoniously and agreeably. . . . For none to move is to yield the ground to the enemies of ecclesiastical order and to sectaries. For only one class friendly to a strong government, to move, is to give the ground to the other extreme party. The

[28] Bentley, *Diary*, III, 89.
[29] Yale Letter, June 15, 1806.

proper course is for all who are friendly to some known and established plan of government and discipline to meet and act in concert.[30]

After the union of the Calvinists and Hopkinsians had been effected, further attempts were made to establish a working basis for a more effective ecclesiastical order. Morse was appointed on numerous committees with this end in view. In 1815, he was made chairman of a special group to "inquire into the history of an original MS. document, found among the papers of Rev. Cotton Mather, containing an answer to the question, 'What further steps are to be taken, that Councils may have their due constitution and efficacy in supporting, preserving, and well ordering, the interest of the Churches in the country?' " [31] The report was made at the 1815 meeting of the General Association and approved the establishment of a form of Consociation. The only definite result of the study was the publication of Morse's report. Thus at every step along the way Morse's efforts to unify the orthodox in a powerful ecclesiastical organization met with failure. He cherished this object until the end of his controversial career and never gave up hope of seeing it realized. However, other attempts along different lines brought more evidence of success.

In 1800, Dwight of Yale and the Federalist Oliver Wolcott urged Morse to unite in the formation of a new paper. The printed proposals expressed his fundamental sentiments and he responded with his characteristic enthusiasm in the venture "to support the Government, morals, religion and state of society in our country in general, and particularly the institutions and estate of society in New England; to defend these on the one hand, and on the other to expose Jacobinism

[30] Sprague, *Life of Jedidiah Morse*, pp. 87–88.
[31] *An Inquiry into the Right to Change the Ecclesiastical Constitution of the Congregational Churches of Massachusetts*, 1816, p. 3.

in every form, both of principle and practice, both of phi-
losophism and of licentiousness." [32] He soon discovered that
the main emphasis of the *New England Palladium* was political, and consequently decided to devote his energy in the
creation of a religious monthly magazine. Here he found a
venture suited more to his desire and ability. The intricacies
of theological systems held little appeal to the "Father of
American Geography." He felt more at home gathering data
and compiling facts than musing over metaphysical subtleties,
or debating political issues. In contrast to the "Divine of
Franklin" and the "cultured liberal of Salem" [33] he was first
and foremost a leader of men and a champion of causes. His
own religion had been settled to his satisfaction before he
entered the ministry. Now he felt it needed only defense and
promulgation. "He had an ardent love for the doctrines of
the reformation, regarding them, however, not so much in an
abstract or theoretic, as in a practical view. He possessed a
fertile imagination, the power of ready thought, and the pen
of a ready writer, and an extraordinary habit of despatch." [34]
Furthermore, his broad contacts on behalf of his geographical labors gave him a fairly accurate picture of the religious
situation of New England.

Popular acceptance of the numerous periodicals of the time
offered Morse the opportunity he needed. He communicated
with his friend Dwight of Connecticut asking his advice.
Dwight replied enthusiastically:

. . . there are men enough and talents enough. Had I eyes, you
would find me at least embarking heartily in the design, and forward-
ing it with something beside mere good wishes. You will find occasion for all your prudence and patience; but, when the war is fairly begun, I expect soldiers will enlist. . . . I enter into all your feelings and

---

[32] Sprague, *Life of Jedidiah Morse*, p. 242.
[33] Nathanael Emmons and William Bentley.
[34] Leonard Woods, *History of Andover Theological Seminary*, pp. 53–54.

interests, as they are mentioned in your letters. I am disappointed in two things which you mention: the union of the Arminians with the Unitarians, and the separation of the Hopkinsians from the Old Calvinists, that is, in the recent controversy. Both (the Arminians and the Hopkinsians) are unwise; for the question concerning the Trinity interests them both equally with the Old Calvinists, so far as they hold their professed doctrines.[35]

It had been Morse's intense desire for some years to unite the old Calvinists and the Hopkinsians and his activity in fostering the General Association had been directed toward this end. The "consistent Calvinism" of the Hopkinsians led this group to be sceptical of his "moderate Edwardean theology" and reluctant to coöperate. Morse saw the wisdom of enlisting the support of this expanding group of Massachusetts Hopkinsians, along with those like-minded and sympathetic Edwardeans in Connecticut personified by Timothy Dwight at Yale. Western Massachusetts, he knew, could be counted on in defense of evangelical religion.

Morse further noticed with regret the growing self-consciousness of the liberal group. He watched their insistent domination grow bolder and more self-confident both at Harvard University and in their magazine, *Monthly Anthology*. Such speculative differences as existed between the Old Calvinists and the Hopkinsians, he considered as minor matters in the impending crisis. He resolved anew to gain their confidence and secure their coöperation. His tactics were consequently based upon this predominant desire for a united front. To effect this he made a strategic move at the start of his magazine in appealing to Leonard Woods to act with him as editor.

Woods was a member of the Essex County Hopkinsian Association and accepted among them as one of their own.

[35] Sprague, *Life of Jedidiah Morse*, pp. 66–67.

He was an intimate and respected friend of Spring at New-buryport, and had been selected by him as one of the editors of their periodical, the *Massachusetts Missionary Magazine*. Woods wrote that "Dr. Morse . . . knew well my views of theology and my character as a minister before he invited me to be a joint editor with him in the *Panoplist*. He knew that in a moderate sense I was a Hopkinsian, but on account of this moderate sense he had chosen me." [36]

Woods's associations, as well as his amiable and cautious character, gave promise of inestimable value to Morse's project. But Woods was reluctant to accept. "As to Dr. Morse's proposal to me," he wrote, "I thank him for the obligation he has conferred. But I must think he shows more friendship than discernment in looking to me." [37] However, after reviewing the statement of the proposed magazine which Morse circulated about April the first, he declared that it "corresponds entirely with my views, and I consented to the proposal of Dr. Morse to be one of its editors." [38]

Thus, with renewed confidence Morse prepared the first issue. He wrote to George Burder of London, June 1, 1805,

Arminianism, blended with Unitarianism, has been gradually increasing in Boston and vicinity for a number of years past, till within a few months their advocates have boldly taken their ground, and are fast assuming the form of a distinct sect. Some of the Hopkinsians, who have become also a sect, seem inclined to vibrate to the opposite extreme. The supporters of the Panoplist take a middle ground, such, we conceive, as the Editors of your Evangelical Magazine occupy. We hope for an amicable coalescence, at a future time, with the great Body of Hopkinsians, who are valuable men. We shall have a struggle,

---

[36] Woods, *History of Andover*, p. 106. For Woods's complete theology and his relation to the Hopkinsians, see Williston Walker, *Ten New England Leaders*, Ch. IX; also, the *Congregational Quarterly*, Vol. I, April, 1859, pp. 105–24, article on Leonard Woods, by Rev. E. A. Lawrence.

[37] *Ibid.*, Letter, April 16, 1805, p. 450.

[38] *Ibid.*, p. 43.

I expect, in order to maintain our ground. But I hope that we shall be enabled to do it, having, as I firmly believe, Truth and its Divine Author on our side. The present crisis has been hastened by the publication of a pamphlet which I sent you entitled, "True Reasons, etc.," which I published in my own defense, as you will perceive.[39]

In June the first issue appeared. Woods wrote to Morse:

Today Panoplist is born. I hope he may grow up and be a good man, the friend of knowledge and religion. I have no food yet cooked for the babe, but have some doing. . . . As far as I have had time to examine Panoplist, I am satisfied. . . . It looks as though the Editors felt able to stand up and look the world in the face. We greatly need the panoply ourselves that we may furnish others. . . . I hope and pray there may not be a spirit of ill-nature or bitterness in the whole Panoplist. It doesn't belong to the Christian armour.[40]

The contrast between the Preface of the *Monthly Anthology* and the statement of purpose in the *Panoplist* is the difference between two religious cultures.[41] One is liberal, "genteel," and primarily literary, while the other is crisp, definite, sectarian. The *Panoplist* statement reads like a stirring battle cry. Its writer is evidently in a state of intense conviction and alarm, and pictures the statement tacked on the door of every New England church as a call to arms. Morse's character and religion were apparent in every utterance:

. . . It is the duty of the friends of evangelical truth and Christian morality, to be "up and doing," to "take unto them the whole armour of God," and with one heart and one soul to "contend earnestly for the faith once delivered to the saints." . . . While the enemy armed with a specious and subtle philosophy, by secret marches were pouring in like a flood upon the Christian world, and threatening it with moral desolation, the Spirit of the Lord, in the fervent prayers, the vigilance

[39] Sprague, *Life of Jedidiah Morse*, pp. 65, 66.
[40] Woods, *History*, pp. 453–54.
[41] See Ch. VII, pp. 85, 86.

76

and active exertions of the faithful followers of the Lamb, hath marvelously lifted up a standard against them. . . . The enemies of the cross of Christ . . . have been valiantly resisted, and their machinations unveiled and disconcerted; yet they are still on the field and in force, embittered by disappointment, and by various artifices and methods of attack are continually endeavoring to accomplish their demoralizing schemes and to effect the overthrow of the Christian religion.[42]

The definite aim of the periodical was "pure truth, flowing from the sacred fountain of the scriptures; nothing of the Shibboleth of a sect; nothing to recommend one denomination of Christians, or to throw odium on another; nothing of the acrimony of contending parties against those, who differ from them; but pure, genuine Christianity, in which all the followers of the Lamb, who are looking for the mercy of the Lord Jesus Christ unto eternal life, can unite with pleasure, as in one great common cause."[43]

Professing to be a "follower of the Lamb," Morse proceeded with his publication with all the characteristics of a lion, carrying practically the entire burden for some time. Consequently, the first few issues revealed much of his attitude and sentiment. The opening article of the periodical was a "Sketch of the Life and Character of Rev. David Tappan, D.D." vindicating this former Hollis Professor at Harvard.[44]

Morse immediately made a bid for the coöperation of the

[42] Preface to *Panoplist*, Vol. I, 1805.

[43] *Ibid.*, Preface.

[44] In a later issue Tappan is criticized: "But it admits a query, whether he [Tappan] used for that purpose [training the students in an adequate knowledge of religion] all the influence which might have been derived from his office, his talents and the high place he possessed in the affection of ministers and students. In some other ways, the energy of his character was exhibited to much greater advantage. His usefulness to the cause of divine truth, it is thought, might, in some instances, have been promoted by a higher degree of resolution, and by measures more decisive. It is doubted, whether he uniformly showed in what high estimation he held the distinguishing doctrines of the gospel." *Panoplist*, Sept., 1805, I, 141.

Presbyterians. He published the report of the committee on the general state of religion exhibited to the General Assembly of the Presbyterian church in the United States of America. Also, in reprinting the "Life of Dr. Samuel Finley" from the Assembly's *Magazine*, he added that

this is a very respectable periodical work published in Philadelphia . . . under the patronage of the Presbyterian Church in the U. S. of America. . . . It is ably conducted. In sentiment it is purely evangelical according to the doctrines of the Reformation, and those contained in the Westminster Confession of Faith, and the Assembly's Catechism. . . . We cordially recommend this work to the attention of our readers, as an able advocate for religious truth, and as an honour to the literary character of our country.[45]

Sermons by Dr. Ashbel Green were described as having "evangelical fervour, sacred dignity and elegance," and containing "riches of divine truth."

Certain British periodicals were recognized. The *Evangelical Magazine* was "highly approved by the friends of vital religion in the United States. . . ." [46] The *Christian Observer and Religious Monitor* (or Scot's *Presbyterian Magazine* of Edinburgh) were "recommended to readers" and articles frequently republished from them. The attitudes revealed in such features of these periodicals as the "Reviews of Books," and "Sermons," "Reports," all indicated the high praise of "revivals in religion" among the orthodox and a denunciation of tendencies toward irreligion among the liberals.

When the "war" was fully begun soldiers began to enlist as Dwight had predicted. Asa McFarland sent a note of encouragement from New Hampshire: "The Panoplist as far as I can learn gives general satisfaction in this quarter. Our

[45] *Panoplist*, I (Dec., 1805), 281.
[46] *Ibid.*, I, 37.

friends here will be pleased to see it decided in the support of the Calvinistic system of doctrine as maintained by the reformers and the primitive Christians of New England." [47] Two thousand copies of the third issue were printed, indicating the widespread popularity of the new monthly. Morse communicated enthusiastically to Dr. Dana that "subscribers for the Panoplist are constantly increasing. It will succeed by activity and perseverance on the part of its able friends, among whom, we reckon yourself. It will be kept on the old ground, that is, on Catechism ground." [48]

"The Panoplist is the only channel through which we can, with effect, communicate such information to the public from time to time, as may be necessary to our purpose," he wrote to Dr. Lyman. " 'Tis the only weapon of the kind which our opposers fear. It is now formidable, and must be made more so. . . ." [49] Words of encouragement came in from England. Morse's friend Wilberforce wrote: "I return you thanks for your new periodical publication, which I have read over with pleasure, and I trust it will be productive of that best species of good which you have in view in instituting it. In times like these let not Christians be lukewarm or inactive in their Master's service, but be ever abounding in the work of the Lord, in every good word and work, varying their efforts as circumstances may require, and judiciously adapting them to the various exigencies which render them necessary." [50] From London he heard from Zachary Macaulay: "I feel no small satisfaction in the establishment of such a work as the Panoplist, and that the Conductors of it should have so favourably noticed the Christian Observer,[51] I shall be very happy to

[47] Yale Letter, Sept. 8, 1806.
[48] Yale Letter, Oct. 17, 1806.
[49] Yale Letter, April 22, 1806.
[50] Sprague, *Life of Morse*, p. 68.
[51] Morse drew upon the *Christian Observer* in certain parts of the Preface.

forward their pious views in any manner which may be in my power. . . ." [52]

As "soldiers enlisted" with Morse in contending for the "faith once delivered to the saints," the enemy was characteristically indifferent. Bentley casually remarked, "Dr. Morse's Panoplist is employed with a host of Pamphlets in the good cause of antiquated Orthodoxy. It is to be hoped their stupidity will work wonders in the reformation from corruption of Christianity." [53] The editors of the *Monthly Anthology* considered its appearance meriting an inconspicuous notice under "New Publications."

From Hopkinsian quarters came serious doubts and fears. The *Panoplist* was viewed with jealousy as a rival of their *Massachusetts Missionary Magazine.* In its behalf, Samuel Austin, one of the editors, pleaded with Woods not to "secede from the Hopkinsian doctrine. It is solid rock. Do not neglect the Magazine. If the Panoplist can live, be it so. But the Magazine must not be forsaken." [54] In the same month that the *Panoplist* appeared, a "Friendly Address" was published in the *Missionary Magazine* urging the Hopkinsians to stand by their publication. "We must defend our standard. This is our Flag. This is the ensign of our disinterested band." [55]

This attitude did not give much encouragement to Morse in his great desire for an "amicable coalescence with the great body of Hopkinsians." In fact he thought it wise to postpone the attempt to unite the *Panoplist* and the *Missionary Magazine* because of the movement toward coöperation for a theological seminary. The two periodicals were not brought together until these two orthodox groups had established a

[52] Sprague, *Life of Morse*, p. 69.
[53] Bentley, *Diary*, III, 184.
[54] Woods, *History of Andover*, p. 453.
[55] *Massachusetts Missionary Magazine*, June, 1805, III, 4.

working basis. Into this task Morse threw his entire energy. In the meantime Woods advised him to maintain a "respectful silence" toward the Hopkinsians "concerning the Panoplist and Missionary Magazine." [56]

[56] Woods, *History of Andover*, p. 459.

CHAPTER VII

MORSE AND THE HARVARD CONTROVERSY

THE redoubtable champion of orthodoxy staged one of his most dramatic battles around Harvard College. As a member of the Board of Overseers and one intensely interested in the New England seat of learning, Morse watched, not only with alarm but with utter dismay, the growing trend toward liberalism. He believed that, if the main source of intellectual and theological leadership should be corrupted with what he felt to be irreligion, then the last blow would have been struck at his cause.

As early as 1797, Freeman, the outspoken Unitarian of Kings Chapel, revealed the way the cultural wind was blowing in Boston and Cambridge. In a letter to a friend he stated:

Though it is a standing article of most of our social libraries that nothing of a controversial nature should be purchased, yet any book which is presented is freely accepted. I have found means, therefore, of introducing into them some of the Unitarian Tracts with which you have kindly furnished me. There are few persons who have not read them with avidity; and when read, they cannot fail to make an impression upon the minds of many. From these and other causes, the Unitarian doctrine appears to be still upon the increase. I am acquainted with a number of Ministers, particularly in the southern part of this state, who avow and publicly preach this sentiment. There are others more cautious, who content themselves with leading their hearers, by a course of rational but prudent Sermons, gradually and insensibly to embrace it. Though this latter mode is not what I entirely approve, yet it produces good effects.[1]

Mr. Lindsay made a present of Dr. Priestley's theological works to the Library at Harvard College, for which, Belsham states, "as a very valuable and acceptable present he received the thanks of the President and Fellows. These books were read with great avidity by the students." [2] Likewise, other books were accepted at Harvard from John Disney, Granville Sharpe, Joshua Toulmin, Richard Price, and other English authors.[3]

That Morse was justified in his alarm is further indicated by his Presbyterian friends. Dr. Archibald Alexander, while visiting Dr. Eckley in 1801, tells of attending the Thursday lecture where

old Dr. Howard delivered a downright Arian sermon; not in a controversial way, but just as if all agreed with him. Indeed at that time all controversy was proscribed by the liberal party. After the sermon I was presented to Dr. Morse, who greeted me cordially, and invited me to Charlestown. A dozen venerable looking clergymen were present, some with fullbottomed white wigs. There is as yet no public line of demarcation among the clergy. One might learn with ease what each man believed, or rather did not believe, for few positive opinions were expressed by the liberal party. Dr. Kirkland was said to be a Socinian, as was Mr. Poplan; and Dr. Howard an Arian. Dr. Eckley had professed to be an Edwardean, but he came out, after my visit, a high Arian. Mr. Emerson a Unitarian of some sort, Mr. Eliot was an Arian, and Dr. Lathrop a Universalist. Dr. Freeman, one of the first who departed from orthodoxy, was the lowest of all, a mere humanitarian. He still used the book of Common Prayer, altered so as to suit his opinions. Dr. Morse was considered a rigid Trinitarian. Dr. Harris of Dorchester, was [declared] a low Arminian, and became a thorough Unitarian. . . . Harvard College was not yet fully under

[1] E. H. Gillett, "Review of American Unitarians," p. 12 (quoted in the *Historical Magazine*, April, May, 1871, p. 236).
[2] *Ibid.*, p. 17.
[3] See Sidney Willard, *Memoir of Youth and Manhood*, II, 117.

Unitarian influence, but was leaning in that direction. President Willard was thought to hold the old Puritan doctrine, but had no zeal for orthodoxy. Dr. Tappan, professor of theology, was in his writings a Calvinist of the school of Watts and Doddridge; a very amiable man; of prepossessing manners. Dr. Pearson was a professor of Hebrew; he was much opposed to Unitarianism, but did not possess great influence. All were for making little of doctrinal differences. As soon as the liberal men had caused this to be settled as a principle, they devised a way to introduce the ablest Unitarians into the college. Even at the time of my visit, all the young men of talents in Harvard were Unitarian.[4]

Young Joseph, son of the venerable and orthodox Buckminster of Portsmouth, was the typical fruit of Harvard at the beginning of the century. In spite of the constant vigilance and training of his father, he left his Alma Mater thoroughly inculcated with the liberal sentiments. He had learned to be a great admirer of Priestley, though not accepting the full implications of his theology. On a visit to the elder Buckminster, Dr. Alexander remarked about the son Joseph, who had just graduated from Harvard; he "was the pride of Harvard" and "was full of anecdotes, such as were current at Cambridge, and which were mostly intended to ridicule evangelical opinions." [5]

This brilliant young man was called to the Brattle Street Church at Boston in the year 1804, before he was twenty-one years of age. His father pleaded with him to reside "a little while with Dr. Morse," [6] in the desperate hope that much of the influence of Harvard would be worn off and his son would be revived in the evangelical truth. But a later letter indicates the attitude toward Morse: "I am sorry," wrote the elder Buckminster, "that Dr. Morse should be unpopular

[4] J. W. Alexander: *Life of Archibald Alexander*, pp. 251–54.
[5] *Ibid.*, pp. 257, 258.
[6] Eliza B. Lee, *Memoir of Rev. Joseph Buckminster*, p. 142.

with any of your society, or that you should feel as if any of the society did not esteem and respect him." [7]

Another factor entered the scene about this time and was destined to play an important role in the impending controversy. This was the establishment of the *Monthly Anthology* —a magazine which provided a means of expressing the sentiments of the liberal group. The picturesque Preface in the first issue presented its object: ". . . we purpose that he [the *Anthology*] shall not be destitute of the names of a gentleman, nor a stranger to genteel amusements . . . his dress and conversation shall borrow mode and graces of the most polished circles in society." [8]

"If he should commit himself to the guidance of unskilful hands, or guideless, add to the number of rash innovations of the present age . . . should he turn . . . heretic in religion . . . or wilfully wrong the meanest individual, we shall immediately spurn him from our presence." [9]

In later issues the editors from time to time indicated their attitude: "They [the editors] are satisfied if they in any way contribute to the mild influence of our common Christianity, and to the elegant tranquility of literary life. They are gentle knights, who wish to guard the seats of taste and morals at home. . . ." [10] "They are not enlisted in the support of any denomination or prejudice; nor are they inspired with the fanaticism of literary crusaders." [11] Toward the close of the *Anthology's* existence, the editors stated that "we claim also this merit, that we have never lent ourselves to the service of any party, political or theological . . . we have never

[7] *Ibid.*, pp. 200, 201.
[8] See M. A. DeWolfe Howe, *Journal of the Proceedings of the Society which conducts the Monthly Anthology and Boston Review*, pp. 6, 7.
[9] *Ibid.*, p. 9.
[10] *Ibid.*, p. 18.
[11] *Ibid.*, p. 9.

courted the suffrage of the great vulgar, nor attempted to enlist the prejudices of the small; have never felt, in any discussion in which we have been engaged that we have had any other cause to serve than that of truth and good learning." [12]

In 1803, the death of Tappan, who was Hollis Professor of Divinity at Harvard, presented the problem of choosing his successor. In the conflict that ensued, the smoldering fires of tension between the liberal and orthodox were fanned into renewed heat. Tappan and Morse were of about the same theological sentiments. "Without pretending to fix the exact point of Dr. Tappan's temperature on the doctrinal thermometer," wrote Ware, "it fell within the somewhat vague range of what had already begun to be called moderate Calvinism. Dr. Morse, who vindicated for him a sufficient though not the highest degree of orthodoxy, sets him down as a Sublapsarian." [13]

At the time of Tappan's election to the Divinity chair in 1793, only one man had opposed the attempts of Morse and his friends to install there a man of their sentiments. Dr. John Clark of Boston, an overseer of the college felt that one of a more liberal mind should have been elected.[14] But the general atmosphere at Cambridge had been greatly changed in the following ten years. William Bentley indicates the liberal point of view at the death of Tappan. On the 28th day of August (1803), he records in his diary:

This day the News reached us that Dr. David Tappan, Professor of Divinity in the University of Cambridge, our favorite seminary, has breathed his last. He was heard with great attention when young. He was flowery, animated and devout. Calvinistic and much alarmed by Illuminatism. . . . He could declaim rather than reason and his

[12] *Ibid.*, p. 24.
[13] William Ware, *American Unitarian Biography*, I, pp. 236, 237.
[14] See Bentley, *Diary*, III, 38.

prejudices would not admit a candid examination. His friends rather loved than admired him, and they loved him more from his innocence than his energy. . . . He could persuade us to love religion, and he lived agreeably by it. But he had not that extensive reading, that powerful research, that luminous method, which gives to instruction its full extent, the generous aid and its best convictions.[15]

Morse foresaw the conflict which was to take place. In a letter to Dr. Lyman, dated December 4, 1804, he wrote: "There is a violent struggle to elect an Arminian professor and President for our university, and avowedly to make it the Arminian College. The choice of Professor will probably be made before this reaches you. I fear and deprecate a revolution in our university more than a political revolution. I pray God in mercy, to prevent both. But we have abused and forfeited Divine favors, why should we expect their continuance? God is long suffering and full of compassion. These attributes only encourage hope." [16] This letter was written the day following the first official meeting of the Harvard Corporation at which the subject was considered. It indicates that Morse may have had some report of the meeting from his friend, Professor Eliphalet Pearson, who championed the cause of orthodoxy in that body.

"Before the long controversy about the choice of a Hollis Professor of Divinity," wrote Willard's son, "I was not aware of the sternness of Dr. Pearson's orthodoxy, so called. About that time I remember his speaking in terms of high commendation of William Wilberforce's 'Practical View of the Prevailing Religious System of Professed Christians.' But I supposed it was the spirit rather than the letter of the writer that roused his enthusiasm and stirred his eloquence; that moved his affections, without imparting new light to religious

[15] *Ibid.*, p. 38.
[16] Yale Letter, Dec. 4, 1804.

dogmas, or changing his views of the radical doctrines of the Gospel."[17] Arrayed with Pearson on the Board was Judge Wendell of whom Willard speaks as a "man of peace" who tried to bring about a compromise between the two contending parties.[18] The Liberals were represented by two well-known Boston clergymen, Dr. Lathrop and Dr. Eliot, along with "the learned and upright Judge Dana of the District Court of Mass."[19] This triumvirate proposed the Rev. Henry Ware of Hingham, as their candidate for the professorship, while the orthodox were anxious to see Jesse Appleton, the minister of Hampton, fill the vacant position.

There is an indication that Morse himself would have liked to have the opportunity of teaching at Harvard.[20] But evidently the orthodox felt that the "cautious" Mr. Appleton would be more acceptable to the Liberals. He was, according to Willard, a "practical and very serious teacher, acceptable to the Orthodox, and I believe, to many who widely differed from them in speculation."[21]

The elder Buckminster wrote to his son stating: "If I were as much of a Hopkinsian on some points as you, my son, are upon others, I should be glad they had thought of Mr. Appleton for Cambridge. I think there is no man so likely to render calm and to keep quiet the two opposite parties, and to preserve Cambridge from becoming the arena of theological discord."[22] "It is well known," says Appleton's biogra-

---

[17] See Sidney Willard, *Memoir of Youth and Manhood*, II, 175.

[18] *Ibid.*, p. 174.

[19] *Ibid.*, p. 195.

[20] "He [Morse] inflamed the controversy by traducing its saintly and revered champions and exponents whose 'resolute and successful purpose that he should not fill the Hollis Professorship of Divinity at Cambridge, nor even dictate who should fill it' was universally believed among the Unitarians to have largely influenced Dr. Morse in the personalities of his course toward them." Edes, *History of the Harvard Church in Charlestown*, 1879, p. 54.

[21] Willard, p. 174.

[22] E. B. Lee, *Memoir of the Rev. Joseph Buckminster and of His Son*, Letter Dec. 31, 1804, p. 201.

pher, "that his views of the most important subjects such as Christ's character and atonement, God's eternal scheme and all-directing providence, depravity and regeneration, the distinguishing nature of religion, and future retribution, were conformed to the views which the founders of the College and the fathers of New England entertained. They were such as are exhibited in the renowned Assembly's Catechism which, for the sake of distinction, has been called the Orthodox or Calvinistic scheme." [23] Sprague ranks Appleton with the Orthodox, "on the ground that he was always in fellowship with them. . . . But I am confident in the opinion, that, when I was with him (1804) he was neither a Calvinist, nor a Trinitarian, in any proper sense of the terms; nor, as I think, to the end of life, though he did believe in a kind of atonement, and a transmitted tendency to evil, which had some affinities with Calvinism." [24]

Henry Ware, the Liberal candidate, has been described as "a man of singularly blended sweetness of temper, austere integrity of conscience and a touching humility of spirit." [25] Morse would have been the logical candidate as a leader of the Orthodox but in opposition to such a character, and in consideration of the liberal basis of judgment, Morse would have had very little chance. It is possible that Morse sacrificed his personal ambition for the sake of the cause he championed. He, no doubt, realized that Appleton's character would compare more favorably with Ware's than would his own and that orthodoxy would therefore stand a better chance of holding Harvard College with Appleton as its candidate.

[23] *Panoplist*, I, pp. 185–92.
[24] Samuel Willard, *History of the Rise, Progress . . . of Rupture in Churches . . . at 1st. Church, Deerfield, Mass.*, Sept. 22, 1857, p. 5. Also, Sprague, *Annals of the American Pulpit*, II, pp. 380–89.
[25] Allen and Eddy, *History of the Unitarians and Universalists*, p. 187.

Morse's deep concern in the matter is further revealed in a letter to Dr. Joseph Lyman of Hatfield:

There is a powerful attempt making to place a Unitarian in the Professor's chair. Firm opposition is made to this unwarrantable measure. The issue hangs in suspense. If the measure be pushed on their side, I see nothing but open war between them and the Calvinists which will seriously affect the usefulness of the University, and the peace of the state. I am very deeply alarmed on this subject. Dangers indeed thicken around us on every side. Heaven avert impending calamities. Will you talk with Governor Strong and Mr. Hasting on the subject? . . . It is no easy matter to rouse men who are devoted to the acquisition or the enjoyment of wealth, to act vigorously in any cause. . . . I am by no means certain that the controversy between Trinitarians and Arians and Socinians will not be revived by this dispute concerning a Professor. It is best to be prepared for such event. I wish that Dr. Lathrop would be prevailed on to write and publish on the subject. Will you persuade him to do it? I think it will be well for you to do the same, and for all able divines to be turning their attention to the subject. I am apprehensive that things are tending to a schism in the congregational interest. It ought to be avoided if possible, and nothing can prevent it but a compromise in the matter now pending before the Convention . . . the portentous situation of the various things hinted at in this letter has probably taken too deep hold of my mind. I would be happy if we could become the vigilant and active Christians, cast all our cares on Him who careth for us. . . .[26]

The subject was discussed at length in the newspapers and social groups. The Orthodox were leading in the offensive and the Liberals were defending themselves. A writer, assuming the name "Amicus," sent an article to the editor of the *Columbian Centinel* of Boston which was published Saturday, November 24, 1804, asking: "Is there not reason to apprehend that some of the Corporation and Overseers are rather inclined to elect Unitarians or those styled rational Christians, who even deny the proper divinity of the Sav-

[26] Yale Letter, Dec. 27, 1804.

iour? . . . It is a time of great declension both in point of morals and sentiments, but the people of Massachusetts, except in few instances, are not so revolutionized and deluded that they will commit their children to the loose and erronious hands of Unitarians for an education." [27] A Liberal promptly replied with an article signed as "Mahew" stating that "your communication is not remarkable for its delicacy, charity or frankness. It reads as if it had been written at the stake of Servetus, and for the honor of our age, I should have rejoiced if it had been consumed in his funeral fire. . . ." [28] Articles by "Paratus," "Fair Play," "X," "Vindex," and others followed in quick succession, mostly representing the Liberal point of view. "Fair Play" objected to the editor's refusal of an article by Calvinus. [29]

It is significant that there was little inclination on either side to be clear-cut theologically rather than "moderate." The theological lines were not yet drawn clearly between the two groups. Each strenuously insisted that it represented the true and orthodox position. Samuel Willard, son of the eminent President, looking back to this period, said that he "remembered, not long before his death, that my father, remarking upon the reputed heresy of Dr. Howard [of the West Church] in the early days of his ministry added, 'He is now as orthodox as the other ministers of his denomination'—not implying thereby, any change in his friend, but a change in the standard of Boston Orthodoxy." [30] A later writer in the *Anthology* also indicated the unconscious change. "It was pointed out by the critic that those who call themselves Calvinistic subscribe to many different systems. Modern Calvinism is not what it was. . . . One class have incorporated

[27] *Columbian Centinel*, Nov. 24, 1804.
[28] *Ibid.*, Wednesday, Nov. 28, 1804.
[29] This was later published in the *Palladium* for Dec. 18, 1804.
[30] Sidney Willard, *Memoirs of Youth and Manhood*, II, 103, note.

with it the doctrines of philosophical necessity, and another many of the leading sentiments of the Arminians, though both are ambitious of being considered as entitled to the name." [31]

When the charge was brought against Ware that he was a Unitarian, his friends replied that he had never professed "the sentiments imputed to him, and that to mention such a thing was a calumny." Indeed, the pretense that his religious principles were unsound, was ridiculed, as one not entitled to serious consideration. "It is well known, it was said, that an alarm has been raised, 'Beware, he is an Arminian! He is an Arian!'" [32]

Time and time again the Liberals insisted that there was no basis for dispute on religious grounds. They held that Ware was just as "sound and orthodox" as any of his opposers. "On religious opinions, I say nothing," wrote Mayhew,[33] "probably I have adopted your speculative creed as my own in most points. In practice, sir, we differ widely." There was the point! Religion for the Liberals had become primarily a system of morals. To the Orthodox this was irreligion. In fact, they associated the mild humanitarian emphases of the Boston divines with the Unitarianism of Priestley and Belsham. The majority of the liberal-minded clergy of Boston and Cambridge, however, had not adopted the Socinian humanitarian view of Christ held by certain of the English Unitarians. When Priestley came to America he was coldly received by the New England Liberals as one not of their kind.[34] Consequently, this group could truly say the charge of Unitarianism against them was a "calumny."

Their appeal was based on a plea for "honesty and free-

---

[31] *Monthly Anthology*, II, 215.
[32] See *Spirit of the Pilgrims*, II, 472.
[33] *Ibid.*, p. 472.
[34] See G. A. Koch, *Republican Religion*, Chap. VII.

dom." "The pontifical power" assumed by their opponents was irksome in a "Free and Christian country." [35] They urged a broad, charitable interpretation of religion rather than a narrow sectarian attitude. They claimed that it is "less important to ascertain what side of subtle and indeterminable controversy he [the candidate] has taken, than to be satisfied that he is a disinterested lover of truth. . . . We wish him moral, pious, faithful, amiable, modest and unassuming." [36]

To the orthodox this attitude was faithless and downright irreligious. They rebuked their opponents for their "indifference" on matters of faith, particularly as to the doctrines of Christ's divinity. The writer named "Vindex" rebuked the Liberals for their constant use of the following lines:

" 'For modes of faith, let zealous bigots fight:
His can't be wrong, whose life is in the right.'
which, though good poetry, certainly is bad divinity." It may be that this is directed especially to William Bentley of Salem, who in defining his religious attitude stated in almost the same words that "the only evidence I wish to have of my integrity is a good life, and as to faith, his can't be wrong whose life is in the right." [37]

Morse and his friends were led by their convictions to bring the issue into clear relief. In the February issue of the *Monthly Anthology,* an article appeared which pointed out that

It seems to be the aim of some persons, abounding more in zeal than in knowledge or moderation, to force their opponents upon one of the horns of this dilemma . . . either to maintain their speculative religious tenets in the publick newspapers, or to pass with the publick at

[35] See articles in *Columbian Centinel.*
[36] *Ibid.*, Saturday, Jan. 26, 1805.
[37] Bentley, *Diary*, I, 98.

large as incapable or timid. The former course of conduct, I hope, will never be pursued, whatever may be the consequences. Timidity or incapacity can only be inferred by those, whose opinions are unworthy of regard. The subscriber is not, assuredly, one of those "who have no preference of one style of Divinity to another"; nor does he even think it a matter of small importance what are the speculative tenets of an instructor of youth; yet he cannot but be of opinion, that it is of less importance, whether the candidates for the vacant chairs of the university be followers of Arminius or of Calvin, of Arius or of Socinus, than that they be learned, able, pious men, capable of diffusing instruction, and anxious, but discharging their duty with fidelity, to approve themselves worthy servants of their great Master. . . . It is very well known, however, that the alarm has been raised, Beware, he is an Arminian! he is an Arian! Feeling as I do, most seriously interested in the prosperity of our Alma Mater, I shall lament, as deeply injurious to her usefulness and reputation, that hour, when her present liberal principles shall be exchanged for subscriptions to Articles of Faith; or what is the same thing, when the belief of a certain speculative system shall be esteemed necessary in him, who aspires to the honorable station of an instructor of her sons.[38]

With this keen sense of rivalry threatening the peace of the College, the members of the Corporation kept postponing a definite decision. Writers jibed them, blamed them, and urged them to an immediate conclusion of the whole affair. Finally, at a meeting on February 7, 1805, by a change of one vote, a majority was maintained for Mr. Ware, and he was duly elected.

The choice of the Corporation had to be confirmed by the Board of Overseers, which was composed of the members of the State Senate, ex-officio, and the Congregational clergymen of Cambridge and nearby towns. Just before this body met to approve or disapprove of Ware's election, Morse wrote the following letter to Dr. Lyman:

[38] *Monthly Anthology*, II, 78, 79.

My extreme fears on account of the portentous aspects of our political affairs are almost swallowed up by still greater fears for our University which is most imminently threatened with a revolution which will deeply and lastingly affect the cause of evangelical truth. The corporation have, at length, by a majority of one, chosen Mr. Ware, and next Thursday the overseers meet to sanction or negative the choice. Decided opposition will be made, I fear, however, not by a majority. I believe Mr. Ware is a disciple of the New School, an enemy to Calvinism in every form. His warm supporters are of this class. Dr. Kirkland of Boston will be pushed for President if the other election is sanctioned, then the revolution will be complete; this ancient fountain will be poisoned, and its streams henceforth be the bane of evangelical religion. These are my fears, I pray God they may not be realized. Vigorous efforts will be made to prevent these evils. Pray, my brother, that they may be successful.[39]

When the subject was brought up at the meeting of the Overseers, on February 14, Morse was one of the leaders who made a "vigorous effort" to prevent the sanctioning of Ware. He was supported by Senator Titcomb, his friend of Cambridge, Holmes, and others. He reëmphasized the points already brought up by Pearson in the Corporation and by the Orthodox in the newspaper articles. It was held that the Board had no evidence of Ware's possessing the qualifications required by Hollis in founding the Professorship, and urged that an inquiry be made into his religious faith to determine the "soundness and orthodoxy" specifically mentioned among those qualifications. Morse further insisted that the candidate should be a Calvinist if he were to be true to the intent of Hollis. He also claimed that Ware was of Unitarian sentiments and consequently his election would be a gross misuse of the funds provided by Hollis.

In spite of these objections presented by Morse and his friends, the Overseers finally voted 33 to 23 in favor of

[39] Yale Letter, Feb. 9, 1805.

Ware. Feeling ran high on both sides. Bentley remarked in his diary that

When the Professor nominated by the Corporation was reported to the Overseers of the University, after some silence, Morse dared to object in the most open manner. And his plea was that the Prof-elect was not a Trinitarian, as the foundation required. The vote obtained in defiance of all the influence of this weak and troublesome man. So that Rev. Henry Weare [Ware] is our Professor of Divinity. This is a great point gained for the best hopes of our college at Cambridge, in the view of the strength of religious parties. It now appears that Morse was willing to put himself off at the head of the opposition among the clergy as Pearson had done in the University.[40]

The matter did not end there for Morse. Shortly after the election he sought to vindicate his position in a detailed publication entitled, "True Reasons on which the Election of a Hollis Prof. of Divinity, in Harvard College, was Opposed at the Board of Overseers, Feb. 14, 1805, Jedidiah Morse." In this pamphlet he embellished the points of the controversy with added evidence and comments to prove his position. Its appearance brought words of praise and encouragement from Morse's many orthodox friends, including the Presbyterians in Connecticut and Philadelphia.[41] But it also aroused the disapproval of the Liberals. Bentley commented:

Dr. Morse cannot leave off writing pamphlets. Now he has done with Illuminatism, he has taken up the College at Cambridge and has published a pamphlet of 28 pages with his name entitled, "True Reasons . . ." The principal argument is that Mr. Hollis was a Calvinist, and his bounty is violated in the choice of Mr. Ware. In answer it is said that Professorships are to give general content on the subject of their appointments. That Mr. Hollis declares his pleasure in the free air of Cambridge. Was a Deacon to Jeremiah Hunt, who was not a Calvinistic minister, and the bounty of the family has been continued

[40] Bentley, *Diary*, III, 141.
[41] See Sprague, *Life of Jedidiah Morse*, p. 64.

independently of Calvinistic purposes. He refers to Mr. Ware's Catechism to prove that he was not in consent with Dr. Watt's. He pleads that the college Seal was "Christo et Ecclesiae." But if reason be allied to Religion Mr. Ware may be as loud a friend to the church as any of his predecessors. The first Professor Wigglesworth was deservedly esteemed. The Son had no qualification for that appointment. Tappan was a devotee of his sect. The Professorship may get new reputation from the last appointment. It must be mortifying to Morse, Pearson, and men of their stamp, that they can rule at Cambridge no longer. A few years more and the University must have become contemptible.[42]

Referring later to the effect of this pamphlet, Morse wrote:

It was then, and has been ever since, considered by one class of people as my unpardonable offence, and by another class the best thing I ever did. One of the former party is said to have declared, soon after its publication, that it was so bad a thing that it would more than counterbalance all the good I had done or should do if I lived ever so long; and one of the other party said, if I had never done any good before I made that publication nor should do any afterward, that single deed would of itself produce effects of sufficient importance and utility to mankind to be worth living for.[43]

The Liberals regretted Morse's attempt to keep the controversy inflamed. One writer in the *Anthology* rebuked him as one "whose celerity and force in arguing are nowise impeded by the decisions of victory. . . . Observe," he says sarcastically, "how aptly and modestly he begins to revive the controversy . . . in which he was so fairly vanquished." [44] Another reviewer wrote that "while men, every way so worthy as the professor-elect are chosen to the instruction and government of our University, we shall have good hopes of the spread of said principles and of the prevalence of real

[42] Bentley, *Diary*, March 31, 1805, III, 149–50.
[43] Sprague, *Life of Jedidiah Morse*, p. 64.
[44] *Monthly Anthology*, II, 492.

orthodoxy." [45] And Morse promptly replied that "you or I must be ignorant of the distinction between an Arminian and a Calvinist," and added, "But, Sir, all of us have not yet grown so wise as to reject all precedents of our fathers on subjects of this kind, as 'worm-eaten authority' of no value. There are still some among us, who venerate their wisdom." [46]

Ware was installed on May 14 amid the approbation of his friends. The *Columbian Centinel* reported that he gave a "pathetic latin oration, much admired by the literary part of his audience." [47] Shortly after this Webber was chosen President in the place of the deceased Willard, bringing the Liberals into complete domination of the college. Morse's dreams of becoming the "Dwight of Harvard" and the champion of evangelical religion at Cambridge were permanently doomed. Apparently the long and heated controversy was brought to a close.

But there was still a rankling within the minds of some because of the "illiberal," "uncharitable," and "sectarian" attacks of Morse and his implication of their "unpopular and erroneous sentiments." In certain respects Morse's battle had not been in vain. His accusations bore severely upon a number of leaders who were accustomed to the respect of the community. An opportunity arose for a few of this dissatisfied group to deal a severe blow to Morse and his influence. Early in his ministry those opposed to his sentiments had tried to cut his power by an attack upon his *Geography*. [48]

[45] *Ibid.*, p. 157.
[46] *Ibid.*, p. 207.
[47] *Columbian Centinel*, Tuesday, May 7, 1805.
[48] "Early after my settlement in this place, during the last half of the year 1789, I was insidiously sounded, as to my sentiments concerning the doctrine of the Trinity; and subsequently gave serious offence to some of my brethren in the Ministry, by preaching a course of sermons on that controverted subject at the Thursday lecture. This was followed by a concerted plan to attack my Geography, which was partially executed in the summer of 1793, by Rev. Dr.

Now the time was ripe to capitalize on his recent defeat over the Hollis Professorship and to permanently clip his wings. Bentley indicates that something of this nature was being considered. "In Boston, some attempts to lessen Morse were to make an honest friend prefix his name to a just ridicule of Morse's impertinence. But the man declined the service." [49] However, the Charlestown pastor claimed that just as he was opposing the election of Ware at Harvard "a story originated in Cambridge from one of the students of the college," accusing him of dishonorably using the material for his book from Miss Hannah Adams' work.[50]

When Morse and his friend Parish published their *Compendious History of New England,* a reviewer in the *Monthly Anthology* severely criticized it with such phrases as: "It is rather suited to the tones of a canting fanatick." "The book smells strongly of sect." [51] It was Morse's belief that if he had not taken the stand he did on the Board of Overseers in reference to Ware's election, and had not published his defense, *True Reasons,* there would have been no controversy with Hannah Adams. He was convinced that the "Controversy, in truth, is a great and important religious controversy, on points which affect the vital interest of Christianity. The affair of Miss Adams, and all other matters of like kind, which have been got up and magnified into importance, have been made incidental merely; means only to an end; weap-

---

Freeman, in a pamphlet which he at that time published, containing 'Remarks' on that work. (That this public vindication of the Trinity, with some other facts of the same nature, particularly the exposure of a mutilated edition of Watt's Divine Songs, occasioned this attack upon my Geography, I had evidence at the time to satisfy my own mind [note].) Opposition to this work has since shown itself in many ways, which it is not necessary here to state." J. Morse, *Appeal to the Public on the Controversy Respecting the Revolution in Harvard College,* p. x (Introduction).

[49] Bentley, *Diary,* III, 163.
[50] J. Morse, *Appeal,* p. 2.
[51] *Monthly Anthology,* II, 542–44.

ons of warfare, fabricated to wound an advocate of the orthodox faith, and through him, to wound the cause which he
advocated." [52]

One may believe that Morse exaggerated his claim and
colored it by his habitually intense religious conviction. But
undoubtedly the growing tension between the sentiments of
the Orthodox and Liberals produced the by-product of personal animosity. The result in Morse's case was particularly
spectacular and effective. Sidney, Morse's second son, who
helped publish the "Appeal" as a complete and detailed vindication of his father, admitted that Morse's "influence in Boston
and its vicinity was, indeed, to a great extent destroyed by it.
. . . Their charge of violating the rights of Miss Adams, as
an author, was made so boldly, reiterated for years so persistently, and countenanced so extensively, that it affected my
father deeply and disastrously, in his property, in his pastoral
and social relations, and in other relations intimately connected with his happiness and usefulness." [53]

Finding himself severely criticized in the *Monthly Anthology*, ridiculed in the newspapers, and often unable to retaliate because these journals were of liberal sentiments,
Morse began to look for some means of defending and cham-
pioning his cause before the public. The controversy sur-
rounding the Professor of Divinity at Harvard had hardly
grown silent when this "Philistic giant, imported from Connecticut" appeared on the scene in another guise.[54]

[52] J. Morse, *Appeal*, p. 179.
[53] Sprague, *Life of Jedidiah Morse*, pp. 276–77.
[54] G. E. Ellis, *Half Century of Unitarian Controversy*, p. 17.

CHAPTER VIII

MORSE AND THE FOUNDING OF ANDOVER

OUT of the "ashes of the ancient Seminary" [Harvard] a Phoenix arose and Jedidiah Morse set it upon its visionary flight. Such was his alarm at the "revolution" in the College and at the increasing boldness with which the Liberals made their claims, that Morse resolved to protect the faith and to strengthen the Christian armor by establishing a theological seminary. This time its "soundness and orthodoxy" would be preserved beyond all question for posterity. "That trick shall not be played again. We will put endowments sacred to the faith where they cannot again be trifled with," was his attitude.[1] However, his former dogmatic confidence had been tempered by his recent bitter experiences and he plotted his course with caution.[2]

He was closely associated in his new plans with Eliphalet Pearson who had likewise been defeated in the cause for which he and Morse had valiantly struggled at Harvard. "I learn from good authority," wrote Bentley, "that in the new arrangements for Cambridge, Pearson was to be chosen the President. Then Morse of Charlestown, was to be offered the

[1] G. E. Ellis, "Discussion of the Andover Theological Questions," in *Boston Daily Advertiser*, Nov. 9, 1882.

[2] Morse's reputation among the liberals was indicated by Bentley: "Dr. Morse proceeds in the full career of his religious and political persecutions. He has attacked parties in the state, he has published Ocean sermons and Illuminati sermons. He has attacked the University and he goes on to reprobate the Clergy whenever they are in the way of his prejudices and wishes." (Bentley, *Diary*, III, 218.)

Professorship of Divinity, but was to resign it and give it to Bates [3] of Dedham. Then Mr. Alden was to be the Professor of Oriental languages. But all are disappointed." [4]

Pearson threw all his interest and energy into his short term as Acting President after Willard's death, but after the election of the liberal Professor Webber, he despaired of longer remaining in the institution. "Such a gloom," he wrote in resigning, "is spread over the University, and such is my view of its internal state and external relation and of its radical and constitutional maladies, as to alarm all my fears and exclude the hope of rendering any essential service to the interests of religion by continuing my connection with it."

"What is to become of us?" wrote Morse to his friend Lyman. "I cannot refrain from weeping over our University. We intend publishing Dr. Pearson's resignation and the addresses of the students and his answers in the next number of the Panoplist. They will interest the public, I think, if we are not destined to fall a prey to the artifices of the adversary. My heart is sometimes ready to sink within me; but I hope never to be left to despair of the cause in which I am engaged. There is considerable said in the circle of a few confidential friends of establishing a Theological Academy at Andover, and of placing Dr. Pearson at the head of it. Such a plan appears to strike forcibly where mentioned." [5]

Pearson's mind seemed ripe for such a suggestion. He communicated his desire to do something about the situation

---

[3] See the Dorchester Controversy in the next chapter.

[4] Bentley, *Diary*, III, 317. Bentley blamed Morse for Pearson's failure: "The Senior Professor Pearson, S. of the Corporation, has been long courting the orthodox party to which he never belonged, and by a sufficient degree of zeal he maintained the friendship of Adams's party in the Commonwealth and then of the Anti-Jeffersonians. By a junction with Morse, in the late election of Professor Ware, he was betrayed into the indiscretions of his party and the Federalists determined that he should never fill the President's chair." (Bentley, *Diary*, III, 219.)

[5] Yale Letter, April 22, 1806.

to Morse: "During this period . . . we have in general thought alike and been concerned in various attempts to do something to retrieve the doctrines and good moral state of our forefathers but with less success than could be wished. . . . Might not much rationally and piously be expected from even a small number of serious, pious and zealous Christians, especially ministers combined together and mutually pledged to each other for the sole purpose of supporting, encouraging and quickening one another in every prudent exertion to save and strengthen the things which remain and are ready to die? The time is short, the period of exertion will soon close. The enemy seems to be gaining ground. Can nothing more be done to arrest his progress? Do be thinking of this and with freedom communicate your thought to your sincere and anxious friend." [6] Morse and his friends had been thinking of this and were reluctant to see a man of Pearson's abilities retire quietly to a farm for the remainder of his days. Consequently, they proceeded with their plans to establish a seminary in which "sound and orthodox" training would be available to students for the ministry.

About this time Morse learned, probably through his friend Woods, that the Hopkinsian leader of Newburyport had been also prompted, by the alarm and threat of the Harvard Liberals, to direct his thoughts toward establishing a theological institution. Spring had hoped to see a Hopkinsian institution under Emmons at Franklin. But the slowness with which this materialized led the energetic Spring to interest one of his wealthy parishioners, William Bartlet, in contributing to a Seminary, probably at Newbury.[7] Morse realized that two theological institutions of an orthodox nature would divide the forces of evangelical religion and pre-

[6] Yale Letter, Sept. 1, 1806.
[7] See Woods, *History of Andover Theological Seminary*, pp. 72–73.

sent a weak front to the liberal attacks. It was his conviction that all the orthodox should unite in one seminary.

In this he was supported by Woods who wrote to him in March:

I am more and more convinced that we can't keep any terms with the Socinian crew. They are not honest. They hate the true gospel and the true God. We have suffered by treating them too well. I think heaven has placed you in the front of the battle against the powers of error and wickedness. The Lord support and guide you, and give you victory. If we can only get all calvinists together, we need not fear. Hopkinsians must come down, and moderate men must come up, till they meet. Then the host will be mighty.[8]

Morse immediately set the machinery in action to create sentiment in favor of uniting the Orthodox of all shades of opinion. It was his dominating purpose to "build a wall as high and as strong as he could against all inroads of all forms of anti-Calvinism." [9] To accomplish this he courted the support of the great body of Hopkinsians, the evangelical Presbyterians of Connecticut and southward, as well as all groups of old Calvinists in his own state. This was to be his "darling object" for about two arduous years. He suggested to Woods that he write a series of articles on the subject to be published in the *Panoplist*. Woods replied:

My general plan is this: to point out boldly yet candidly, fearlessly yet modestly, the evils of the times, the evils which affect our Zion, both ministry and churches; to display the defects in the present mode of preaching, the awful neglect of those gospel truths which animated our forefathers, which furnished the groundwork of the reformation, which have overset the thrones of heathen idolatry and reformed the world; to show the evils of disunion, to mourn over the desolations of our churches in point of discipline and in point of godliness, to notice the contempt of creeds, to give a broad hint at the unscriptural, illiberal

[8] Yale Letter, March 15, 1806.
[9] E. A. Park, *The Associate Creed of Andover Theological Seminary*, p. 90.

spirit of "liberality"; to show what is wanting to beautify Zion, to make the grand conclusion this; that a theological academy on the orthodox plan is needed—that is, is loudly called for by the state of our ecclesiastical affairs; that we must have one, if we would transmit uncorrupt Christianity to posterity.[10]

The interest of the moderate Calvinists centered upon Phillips Academy at Andover as the most suitable situation for the proposed institution. Morse, as a Trustee of the Academy (1795–1826), was well acquainted with its purpose of promoting "true piety and virtue." The officers and trustees were all Calvinists "of the anti-Hopkinsian school, with the exception of three or four laymen, whose relations were with the party afterwards known as Unitarians." [11] Furthermore, it was the original intention of the founders of the Academy that eventually a theological institution should grow out of the school.[12]

Another favorable factor was the large gift of Samuel Abbot toward the establishment of theological training at Andover. Abbot had been a prosperous merchant in Boston, and after retiring to Andover had become a Trustee of the Academy the same year that Morse was elected. Theologically, he was of Morse's sentiments, speaking of himself as a "middle man, meaning that he did not go to the extremes of Hopkinsianism on the one hand, and was no Arminian on the other,—but . . . was a Calvinist after the model of the Assembly's Shorter Catechism." [13] After the controversy at Harvard, Abbot, by a codicil of his will, revoked his large bequest to Harvard and bestowed it upon Phillips Academy for a theological professor of "sound and orthodox, Calvinis-

---

[10] Woods, *History of Andover Theological Seminary.* April 29, 1806, p. 458.

[11] Andover, *Memorial of the Semi-centennial Celebration.* L. Bacon's *Commemorative Discourse,* p. 19.

[12] Woods, pp. 449, 450.

[13] Andover, *Memorial,* Stearn's Commemorative Discourse. Note on pp. 151–52.

tic principles of divinity." All of these facts drew the attention of the moderate group to Andover as the logical place for their proposed institution.

On July 10, 1806, a group voluntarily met to talk over definite plans. Morse, being present, was appointed with four others to draw up a constitution for the institution. "It was thought wise and prudent," he later wrote, "to lay the foundation of the Institution on so broad a scale, as to embrace, if I may so speak, all shades of Calvinists—or all who approve the Assembly's Catechism or the Doctrines of the Reformation, in hope that time and friendly intercourse and discussion would bring all together on some middle ground. With these views it was intended that the Professors should be selected from the several shades so that the confidence of each might be secured by an equal representation." [14]

Morse had his mind set to suggest Woods as professor because of his contacts with the Hopkinsians. He urged Woods to sound that group out on the possibility of their joining in. Consequently, Woods visited Emmons at Franklin and wrote to Morse reporting the results:

As to the college, I think he will co-operate with all his might, and other influential men of his stamp, if they can see that Hopkinsians are not neglected and trampled upon in the plan and direction of the Institution. He is pleased with the idea of a College, . . . which all on orthodox side shall join and support. We talked of having an equal representation of every class of orthodox minsters in the constitution and guidance of the institution. Something like this will be a necessary condition of union in the College. [15]

This was almost beyond Morse's expectations. He replied enthusiastically: "I am greatly encouraged to hope that a cordial union, so devoutly to be wished by all good men, may

[14] Yale Letter, Nov. 18, 1807.
[15] Woods, *History of Andover Theological Seminary*, Letter, Oct. 17, 1806, p. 461.

yet be effected. Talk with brother Austin on the subject. Its importance magnifies the more it is contemplated. Call not the Institution a College but a Theological Academy. The idea is to admit young men into this school who have education at some of our Colleges. I believe a plan can be formed, which shall meet the views and feelings of all evangelical men. There is no wish to neglect or to put in the background the Hopkinsians, but to have them unite on generous principles. It appears to me probable, that we must very soon take open and decided ground. . . ." And as Morse continued, the motive and conviction of the man stood out: "I have hope that if such a union can be cordially effected, and the evangelical strength of Massachusetts concentrated, we might yet bring about a counter revolution in our University, through the instrumentality of the Legislature, by an alteration of Charter, and a new Board of Overseers. Keep this idea in your own bosom. It occurred to my own mind, for the first time this evening." [16]

On Monday evening, March 16th, 1807, Woods was invited by Dr. Spring to meet with Bartlet and Brown at the Newburyport parsonage.[17] There he was informed of the plans of the Hopkinsians to proceed with the establishment of their own academy at his own pastoral charge in West Newbury, and with himself as Professor of Theology. Bartlet and Brown pledged their generous financial support and Spring seemed assured of help from Norris at Salem.

The following day Woods went to Charlestown to consult with Morse on business concerning the *Panoplist*. He told of the meeting the previous evening and of the definite plans

---

[16] *Ibid.*, Letter, Oct. 21, 1806, pp. 462, 463.
[17] Woods, in his *History of Andover Theological Seminary* dates this meeting "the later part of the year 1806." (See p. 73.) Correspondence points to the fact that Sprague is probably right in the above date; see Sprague, *Life of Jedidiah Morse*, p. 98.

of Spring. "This information, under the circumstances," wrote Woods, "almost overwhelmed him with a deep sense of the wonderful providence of God. Here was opened to him another, and an entirely new page in the book of God's dealings with the hearts of men." [18]

Morse probably saw the opportunity of uniting the generous gifts of the Hopkinsians with those of Abbot, and of thus providing a strong institution. He told Woods of the mature plans of the Andover group and impressed upon him the necessity of uniting the two proposed theological institutions in one. In writing to Lyman at a later date he remarked: "prompted doubtless by our efforts, the Hopkinsians projected a similar institution. The property pledged to such an institution and the promptness with which they acted, alarmed us. We deprecated the evils of two institutions and the fixed divisions which must be the consequence among the orthodox clergy and churches in the commonwealth." [19]

Morse decided that it was the time to act and to unite the Hopkinsians with the moderate group. He communicated Woods's information to the Andover gentlemen and found them willing to have the Hopkinsians join with them. Consequently, Morse immediately visited Spring and presented his plan. The reply was most discouraging. Spring wrote to Woods presenting his views:

. . . alas, what will become of the Academy if we connect ourselves with men who think differently relative to the method of doing good, and will justify themselves in contracting our influence as soon as they possibly can without embarrassing themselves? Surely they don't wish us to make a junction for the sake of increasing the Hopkinsian interest. They are not so disinterested as all this. No; they are not afraid we shall lose influence by our Institution; but they desire coalition to help themselves. I am willing to admit that they believe we shall lose noth-

[18] Woods, p. 77.
[19] Yale Letter, Nov. 18, 1807.

ing by the connection, at least in the outset. But for God's sake, do we not know, that we can make more uniform ministers in a solitary state, than we can under many restrictions and embarrassments which will be inseparable from the coalition. Have we the least reason to expect success among those who will not give up the half-way covenant, and are forever pleading for the duty which pertains to the best actions of sinners? We cannot part with the advantages of our Academy for any prospect which presents from the union proposed. . . .

. . . we can live in peace at Newberry, but at Andover we cannot, at the present day, unless we relinquish our darling object in Theology. For they have no thought of being converted now.

Then in a personal appeal to Woods he continued:

Only, Brother Leonard, spend as much time in the appropriate studies of divinity for the Academy this year, as you have the last for the Panoplist, and you will feel very differently. If we, any of us, hanker to be under Andover authority, let us read with attention Samuel's address to Israel when they wanted a king. If we must be hewers of wood and drawers of water, let us do the work at home.[20]

The prospect for union seemed, indeed, very doubtful. In the ensuing debate, Morse used every means available to accomplish his purpose. "I had to plead," he told a friend, "as for my life; I told them [the Hopkinsians] that heresy was coming in, destructive to us both,—I wanted all good men to join in resisting the common foe. Now was the time; our differences were not fundamental. If we establish two seminaries now, the discord will be perpetual in our churches; and if cutting off my right hand could prevent such a disaster . . . I would gladly have it done on the spot."[21]

The conflict was further dramatized in Leonard Woods's personal regard for both Spring and Morse. It was evident that he was attracted to each of these two strong personalities

---

[20] Woods, *History of Andover Theological Seminary*, pp. 471–72.

[21] L. Withington, "Essay on Vibrations in Theology," in *Contributions to the Ecclesiastical History of Essex Co. Mass.*, p. 395.

because of a certain similarity between them. The debate in Woods's mind revolved around which of these two he should follow. For some time he tried to straddle the question but states that "the conflict in my mind was terrible. I was like the waves, driven of the wind and tossed." [22]

Spring appealed to Woods: "Are you willing that by your standing still, as you express it, we must lose our inestimable object? We must know your preference in this attitude of things . . . if you now prefer, all things considered, either the coalition or the Seminary before the Newbury Academy, we must make new arrangements, which will however be attended with less advantages than the first." [23]

The thought of being separated from his friend Spring was "insupportable" and the personal appeal touched his heart so deeply that he told Spring that he would go along with him on his plans. But he had no sooner made the decision than Parish and Pearson visited him and persuaded him to withhold definite action. Morse immediately communicated with him and received the following reply:

Your letter excites a train of emotions which I cannot describe. My intimate and happy friendship with you for two years has given me abundant proof of the sincerity, the candor, and the tender piety of your heart. I know how you feel. Your soul is wounded with the divisions which appear among Christians and ministers. You pant for union and love. It is your favorite cause. You plead for it with God, and with his people. But your heart bleeds that so little can be done. Your bleeding heart, dear sir, makes mine bleed. Your letter has given Mrs. Woods and me many sighs and tears. Oh, that I could say anything to afford consolation on the great subject. I have written several times to Mr. Spring; have let him know how sincerely and ardently I desire union, and the reasons for it in my mind. The distinct Institution here is as much his object, as the union scheme is yours. My mind has been in the utmost perplexity and distress most of the week. Some

[22] Woods, *History of Andover Theological Seminary*, pp. 79–80.
[23] *Ibid.*, p. 472.

views of the subject are animating; many views of it excite anxious feelings; and many, very many, humble me. . . . But what can I do in this trying situation? I would ask you, as a father, to advise me. . . . I thank you with all my heart for the wish you express, that our personal friendship may be preserved unimpaired. It is one of my dearest wishes and hopes. May God prevent anything which would interrupt that intimacy, which has been to me so pleasing and so profitable.[24]

Evidently, Woods decided to throw his lot in with Morse for he communicated to his Charlestown friend that from now on he would use all his efforts in favor of the union. He did not wish to give up his friendship with Spring but made up his mind to use his influence in persuading him to join in the union. He agreed with Morse that the Hopkinsian leaders would never yield on any essential point and knew that if his coöperation was to be secured he would have to be assured of maintaining the Hopkinsian sentiments. To this end Morse and Woods worked hand in hand—the one conciliating the Andover group, the other the Hopkinsians. When he was among the moderate Calvinists Woods praised their sentiments and when with the Hopkinsians he assured them of his "consistency."

In May, Woods wrote to Spring:

I never felt more strongly attached to Hopkinsianism than now. I am more and more convinced that this system of religious sentiment and administration is the nearest of all existing systems to the apostolic standard; and in the hands of wisdom and prudence, the most likely by far to do good to the souls of men. I have embraced the system with deliberation, and in full view of all the evils to which Hopkinsians are liable. . . . My aim is to imitate your example. I mean to do all I can to promote the cause of gospel truth in its most distinguishing form. I mean to advocate the religion in substance which distinguished New England; which religion you have so highly applauded in your late publications. If this cannot be done decidedly and in earnest, I retreat.[25]

[24] *Ibid.*, Letter, April 5, 1807, pp. 475–77.
[25] Gardiner Spring, *Personal Reminiscences*, I, 312, 314.

But the Hopkinsian opposition was decided and almost immovable. Unless concessions were granted in their favor they would withdraw and take their rich gifts to Newbury. On one occasion at a meeting with Morse and others, Nathanael Emmons "rose up against the proposed union." He later said that "the conference closed, and I rode home, fully satisfied that the Coalition was dead." [26]

At this particularly dark period, Woods decided to bring the pressure of his friendship to bear. In a lengthy plea for a united front he wrote to Spring:

Respecting the nature and design of a Theological Institution my views have perfectly harmonised with yours. I consider thorough consistent Calvinism to be Divine Truth. And when I name Calvinism, I mean the system which the most enlightened, and respectable Hopkinsians embrace. For many years, as you well know, I have had an increasing conviction of the excellence and importance of that system; and never more than now. The influence of thorough Calvinism is, in my apprehension, essential to the prosperity of the Church and the Nation. A theological Academy, which should not promote that system of doctrinal and practical religion, I should consider a Divine judgment rather than a blessing. . . . But let it be considered that the spirit of the times, particularly the late management of Harvard College, has brought those who were on the old middle ground, to more consistent feelings. They acknowledge their past errors and have come up much higher in orthodoxy. And there seems an evident tendency in the events of Providence towards one, and only one grand division. . . . It cannot be conceived that Hopkinsians would have low ground in the Seminary. If I had any apprehensions that they would, I should not have another favorable thought of union.[27]

This great appeal had its effect even though Woods felt somewhat guilty in his representations. He explained to Morse that "I seized everything which I thought would influence their minds. Some of the arguments and observations

---

[26] Park, *Memoir of Emmons*, p. 207.
[27] Woods, *History of Andover Theological Seminary*, pp. 482–87.

when perused by you, will need candor. I send the letter in full expectation that you will show it to no one, nor mention anything in connection with my name. Lay it aside safe from every eye." [28] He knew the disastrous results if that letter should be seen by the Andover group. He confessed to Morse that "My exertions went to the extent of propriety. . . . But you need not think it strange if you find I have given serious offense to some with whom I have been most intimate." [29] He justified his actions because of the "vast magnitude" of the undertaking and under a "sense of duty" he believed the "Lord directeth his steps." [30] To Woods, this object of conciliating the Hopkinsians and bringing about their union at Andover was no less than a question of "life and death." [31]

When Abbot began to suspect the Hopkinsian leanings of Woods, Morse suggested that Woods pay the gentleman a visit and ease his mind. So successful was Woods that the Esquire said, "I shall esteem you my firstborn son," and offered him a salary of one thousand dollars a year for the rest of his life. Woods commented that "I am happy to think it will be easy to please him, without deviating from duty." [32] Furthermore, he wrote to Morse, explaining that "as you were so solicitous to give satisfaction to Esquire Abbot and to remove the objections so vigorously urged from various quarters, I was led to speak with more freedom, than was decorous, on my own religious views, and to represent everything in as satisfactory a light as I honestly could. All this when discreetly used among a few friends, who enjoyed each other's entire confidence, was attended with no danger, be-

[28] *Ibid.*, p. 493.
[29] *Ibid.*, p. 490.
[30] *Ibid.*, p. 490.
[31] *Ibid.*, p. 514.
[32] *Ibid.*, p. 517.

cause everything was taken in its proper connection, and construed candidly and honourably." [33]

In conference after conference and in the dealings between the two groups seeking to unite, the correspondence of that time reveals that the moderate Calvinists yielded before the definite and insistent demands of the Hopkinsians. Largely through Morse and his two friends, Pearson and Woods, arrangements were made whereby the Hopkinsians could unite without losing anything vital to their beliefs. Woods pleaded to Morse: "Now if it should come to pass, that you and Dr. Pearson are called upon to do even more than you at first contemplated in the way of condescension, and in making sacrifices;—I trust you will embrace the precious opportunity of honoring the Redeemer and promoting His cause." [34] Again Woods wrote: ". . . use all your influence to prevent suspicion and difficulty on your side"; and in reference to the Hopkinsians, "give them what they want at the outset, if they are reasonable. There will be no danger. All will be quiet. A little experience and cooperation will remove jealousy." [35] "Show a readiness to coalesce in ANY proper way, and to attend with patience and candor to any mode of union, which they may propose. . . . The condescending, healing, uniting spirit which you and your associates have showed, has done much toward melting their hearts and preparing them to harmonize." [36]

Morse was called upon many times to placate the old Calvinists. Dr. Dana, an ardent anti-Hopkinsian, objected to the preference shown toward them in certain dealings. Morse wrote to him confidently: "Be assured, my friend, there is

[33] Woods, *History of Andover Theological Seminary*, pp. 563–64.
[34] *Ibid.*, p. 492.
[35] *Ibid.*, p. 500.
[36] *Ibid.*, pp. 512, 513.

no real danger of a predominate Hopkinsian influence." [37]
When the Hopkinsians threatened to balk at the Assembly's
Creed, Morse and Pearson assured Spring that any creed he
and the Hopkinsians would draw up would be approved by
the Andover group.[38] Later, Spring and Woods drew up
their Hopkinsian creed after consulting Emmons, and Morse
proved true to his promise. The Andover group trusted
Morse and Pearson implicitly and left most of the details of
providing the conditions of union to their judgment.

The Hopkinsians insisted upon choosing their own professor of theology considering this as the most important de-
partment in the new institution. Inasmuch as Woods was their
candidate, Morse, with Pearson's aid, persuaded Mr. Abbot
to appoint him. Thus, at every step along the way, the
Charlestown pastor was one of the directing influences in the
final consummation of the union. By bringing Dwight of Yale
upon the scene and having him appointed as one of the Founders, he affiliated the new institution with the great body
of Connecticut Congregationalists. And, finally, to clinch a
working relation with the Presbyterians, he was probably the
determining factor that brought Griffin to the seminary as one
of its first professors.[39]

These transactions were not brought about without the opposition of the Liberals. The few Trustees of Phillips Academy who held Unitarian views withdrew from the confer-
ences when union with the Hopkinsians seemed assured. But
they did not go without a thrust at the result. A strong and
bitter attack was printed in the *Monthly Anthology* by
Thacher.[40] Bentley commented:

[37] Yale Letter, Oct. 19, 1807.
[38] See Woods, *History of Andover Theological Seminary*, p. 99.
[39] *Ibid.*, p. 599; also Sprague, *Life of Jedidiah Morse*, pp. 108–9.
[40] See *Monthly Anthology*, 1808, pp. 17 ff.

This review clearly proves that this Institution [Andover] is indeed Jesuitical and the Calvinists have been made to play into the hands of the Hopkinsians, who when strong enough undoubtedly intend to usurp the grounds and assume sovereign authority. The proof is adequate enough. The basis of the Calvinist institution is the Assembly's shorter catechism, says the founder. The Creed has so much of that Catechism as agrees with Hopkinsianism and no more, and the language conforms to the Hopkinsian system. This the Reviewer unequivocally proves from the Creed, which it repeats and properly italicises. The Jesuitical Scheme is most justly exposed to the World.[41]

But Morse was triumphant. "The camp of the enemy is alarmed," he wrote to Dwight, "they are awake, and every engine of opposition is in requisition. But we are better fortified and are stronger than they imagine. The Union in the Theological Institution and in Panoplist and Magazine makes us powerful and enables us to look them in the face boldly." [42]

When the main difficulties between the Hopkinsians and Calvinists had seemed to be sufficiently surmounted, Morse had seized the time as ripe to unite the periodicals of the two groups. Woods talked to Spring and secured a favorable attitude.[43] But the actual transaction was delayed for a time by a fear of disturbing the union in the Seminary. By clever manipulation, Morse, however, managed to consummate the union of the two magazines. At the close of the Missionary publication the editors stated: ". . . we received an affectionate invitation from our friends, the editors of the Panoplist, to unite with them in a joint publication. The offer was seriously considered by the Missionary society and cordially accepted." [44]

[41] Bentley, *Diary*, Dec. 18, 1808, III, 403.
[42] Woods, *History of Andover Theological Seminary*, p. 597.
[43] *Ibid.*, p. 575.
[44] *Massachusetts Missionary Magazine*, V, 480.

The 28th of September was a day of profound rejoicing for Jedidiah Morse. He saw his "darling object" realized in spite of what seemed insurmountable difficulties. Notice of the services appeared in the *Panoplist:* "This day the Theological Institution established in this town was opened with the following appropriate solemnities:—The Morning Exercises commenced with Prayer by the Rev. Mr. French. This was followed by an Historical Summary of the rise and progress of Phillips Academy, by Dr. Pearson. After this the Constitution of the Theological Academy was read by Dr. Pearson, the Statutes of the Associate Founders, by the Rev. Dr. Morse, and the Additional Statutes of the Founders, by Rev. Mr. Dana, of Newburyport. . . ." And in the afternoon service, "the Right Hand of Fellowship" was given to Pearson at his ordination, by Dr. Morse. "The Assembly, convened from various parts of our country, on this novel and interesting occasion, was numerous and highly respectable. . . . The auspicious commencement of an Institution, so important to the interests of religion and our country, will, we hope, prove a bright morning of a prosperous day." [45]

The enthusiasm of the Orthodox was reflected in Morse's words: "Singular in the history of our country and interesting in a high degree to the friends of the Redeemer, are the transactions of this day. A new era in our churches now commences; and events may be expected to follow of incalculable moment to their purity and prosperity. A new Institution, the off-spring of Christian liberality, broad and scriptural in its foundation, richly endowed, consecrated to the interests of Evangelical truth, rises to bless our country." [46] While to Pearson he stated: "The Lord hath prospered and, we confi-

[45] Sprague, *Life of Jedidiah Morse*, p. 107; *Panoplist*, Sept., 1808.
[46] Collection of *Documents of Andover Theological Seminary*, p. 35.

117

dently trust, will prosper our Institution, which you have been eminently instrumental, with others, in raising." [47]

In contrast to the optimism of Morse and his friends was the remark by Bentley in his diary, indicating the apparent indifference of the Liberals toward the Seminary: "[This] day appointed to open the Theological Institution at Andover," he wrote. "I have not heard the subject mentioned this day so that it is to be presumed no general interest is taken in this transaction." [48] However, many of the liberal group were roused by the establishment of the institution.[49] A sharp article appeared in the *Monthly Anthology* ridiculing Morse and his colleagues at Andover. "The immediate agency of heaven is no longer discerned," claimed the critic, ". . . the beautiful fabrik of providential favour is totally overthrown, even by the candour of Dr. Morse, one of the most zealous favourers of the Institution. It is really a pity, that the Doctor [Pearson] who delivered the historical sketch of the Theological Institution, was ignorant of its history." [50]

[47] *Ibid.*, p. 35.

[48] Bentley, *Diary*, III, 386.

[49] A later note in Bentley's *Diary* revealed a growing concern in liberal minds about the rising influence of the Hopkinsians. "The singular history of the Sect called Hopkinsian seems now to have reached a point from which we can conjecture their resources and their designs. Dr. Dwight early appeared in Connecticut against the present administration. Dr. Emmons of Franklin followed him in his Jeroboam, and Morse echoed near Boston. The present posture of affairs discovers the progress of influence. Dr. Eckley appears in Boston, Spring in Newbury, and the exile from Fitchburg, who was expelled for his violence, Worcester of Salem, dared last Sunday to compare the friends of the administration to Ahab's lying prophets. Such is the combination and to complete the plan, the new college at Andover is to give public stamp to all who are to be promoted as friendly to their interest, and this party in the church are attempting to ride into power upon the shoulders of the Opposition to the government in Massachusetts. The facts are so evident, distinct and conclusive that even the Opposition in Boston are alarmed, as they wish no religious establishment at present which is an enemy to religious moderation. The success of the review of the Andover labour proves this fact as to the better informed citizens of the denominated Federal party. The very indifferent parts of the State which follow their leaders are of no consequence but as they prove the fact of Hopkinsian influence." Bentley, *Diary*, III, 412.

[50] *Monthly Anthology*, III, 686.

The extent to which the feeling of tension between the liberals and orthodox had developed was clearly revealed in a later defense of the above criticism. In the March, 1809, issue of the *Monthly Anthology* a writer stated,

. . . we found that the person employed by the associate founders had contrived to omit one of the standard doctrines; and to introduce, expressly at least two of those doctrines, which the Hopkinsians add to Calvinism, as it appears in the catechism; and indirectly, under the cover of general and ambiguous terms, nearly all the rest of their peculiar tenets. The inference which we drew from this fact, we are unwilling to state, though we acknowledge that we saw it must be this:—that the persons employed by the original founders, and who were bound to prevent any departure from their intentions, were either through ignorance outwitted by those employed by the associate founders; or else that they must have been unfaithful to the trust committed to them.[51]

The defense concluded by pointing out:

We are desirous of reminding those men, who are attacking our friends, invading the tranquility of our churches, and attempting to revive the exploded absurdities of the dark ages, that the friends of rational and scriptural religion, though enemies of theological polemicks, are not so, because their antagonists have nothing vulnerable in their system. . . . We attack them not because they are Hopkinsians, and not because they are Calvinists, but because their conduct and their principles, we believe all honest Calvinists and Hopkinsians ought to unite in condemning. . . . It stands on record against the institution, and all the waters of the ocean can never wash out the stain, that it has been made what it is, by perverting the pious liberality of well-meaning devotion, and sacrificing the first principles of protestantism to the gratification of the unholy ambitions of aspiring heresiarchs.[52]

No doubt there was a basis of fact on which the Liberals grounded their accusation of Morse. Unquestionably, he compromised on matters of theology, indicating that his con-

[51] *Monthly Anthology*, March, 1809, p. 197.
[52] *Ibid.*, p. 205.

victions had been tempered by his own bitter experiences. However, to Morse, theology was not of primary importance, and he sacrificed his moderate views in the interest of establishing what he believed would be a bulwark against the growing Unitarian influence. He considered the final realization of an orthodox theological institution as the masterpiece of his career. Even though his friend Pearson later lost faith in him [53] and expressed his dissatisfaction with the result at Andover, still, Morse ardently cherished the institution as a child of his own, until the end of his days. The seminary grew to be a powerful factor in New England's religious life and was thus a monument to Morse's efforts.

[53] Pearson felt that Morse had "sold out" the Calvinists to the Hopkinsians. In the strained feeling that resulted between the two leaders, Leonard Woods again assumed the task of arbitration. "Your feelings respecting Dr. Pearson," he wrote to Morse, "are wrong as they possibly can be. . . . Time will show you, eternity will show you that Dr. Pearson is as he was. And there has been nothing but a small difference of judgment, respecting the mode of union." Woods, *History of Andover Theological Seminary, Letter,* Dec. 28, 1808, p. 327.

CHAPTER IX

THE SPLIT IN THE CONGREGA-TIONAL FELLOWSHIP

EVENTS transpired rapidly in bringing about the ultimate separation of the Orthodox and the Liberals in the Congregational churches. A reverence for the sacred history and traditions of their common fellowship caused each group to postpone the definite split in the constant hope that the other would be converted. But, instead of conversion, the lines of demarcation grew more clearly defined largely because of the insistent demands of the Orthodox.

From the beginning of his ministry, Morse had tried to expose the differences between his evangelical religion and the liberal sentiments of his Boston friends. Every controversy into which he threw his energies was partly motivated by this desire. His alliance with the Hopkinsians quickened to intense activity his "exclusive" convictions. He now found that the "consistent Calvinism" of his allies could more easily be openly championed than his former "moderate Calvinism." The militant stage into which liberalism developed challenged Morse to a life and death struggle.

The brilliant young Buckminster wrote to his Unitarian friend, Mr. Belsham of England explaining the situation as follows:

Do you wish to hear anything of American Theology? I can tell you that, except in the little town of Boston and its vicinity, there cannot be collected from any span of one hundred miles, six clergymen who have any conception of rational theology, and who would not shrink from the suspicion of anti-trinitarianism, in any shape. . . . It is the prevailing idea, all over the United States, that the clergy of Boston are little better than Deists. . . .[1] The State of Connecticut, the greater part of Massachusetts and New Hampshire are filled with what we call Hopkinsian clergymen, or the followers of Jonathan Edwards, and others (especially Dr. Hopkins), who pushed the first tenets of Calvinism only to their natural consequences. A new theological institution, under the direction of ministers of their description, has just been endowed and opened within thirty miles of Boston; its funds are derived from the extraordinary munificence of three or four well-meaning men, who think to support the cause of orthodoxy, which has been very much declining under the influence of good sense and liberal ministers. However, the most bigoted and exclusive spirit of Calvinism seems now reviving, and, perhaps, gaining ground, even in Boston. I have been for many months, exposed to some of its deadliest shafts, in consequence of a little collection of Hymns, unorthodox, not heterodox, which I have made for the use of my society. However, we shall stand our ground very firmly, in Boston.[2]

And Buckminster added ominously, "We are as yet independent in Massachusetts; and though with some inconveniences retain our old Congregational connexions, subject to no Platform, subscribers to no articles, and united only so far as we please with one another, exchanging with whom we please and acting with those only with whom we find we can best agree. But there is, among us, an increasing party of Calvinists and Hopkinsians, who wish to promote a more exclusive union, and who will, therefore, form a schism in our Congregational connexion and separate from us, and probably send delegates to the General Assembly. They are not yet the majority in our State, and it is much hoped they never will."[3]

[1] E. B. Lee, *Memoir of the Rev. Joseph Buckminster*, Letter, Feb. 5, 1809, p. 593.
[2] *Ibid.*, p. 335.
[3] *Ibid.*, pp. 596–97.

On public occasions there was still an intimate coöperation between the Liberals and Orthodox at the time Buckminster wrote. At the ordination on the 18th of May, 1808, of
Joshua Huntington as colleague pastor with Joseph Eckley
in the Marlborough Street church of Boston, Morse preached
the sermon, Dr. Lathrop gave the charge, Mr. Channing extended the fellowship of the churches, and Mr. Lowell closed
with prayer. "The exercises were devout and animated; and
afforded high satisfaction to the numerous auditors assembled on the occasion." [4] But there was an undercurrent of tension in the meeting. Lathrop urged the young preacher to
"preach the word, the pure word, not corrupted with the
false reasonings or traditions of men." Channing invited him
to "share with us the toils and successes of a ministry, more
honorable in our estimation than the empire of the world; a
ministry, established by the Prince of Peace for the universal
diffusion of truth, holiness and love." He added to the congregation: "May no root of bitterness spring up and trouble
you. Peace be within these walls. Behold how good and how
pleasant it is for brethren to dwell together in unity." [5]

Timothy Dwight was to have preached the sermon on this
occasion but was taken ill on the road from New Haven and
Morse stepped in and preached in his place. As a result his
statement reveals his sentiment more clearly than if he had
had time for a studied preparation. He took as his text,
II Corinthians 4:2: "But we have renounced the hidden
things of dishonesty, not walking in craftiness, nor handling
the word of God deceitfully; but by manifestation of the
truth commending ourselves to every man's conscience in the
sight of God." After a defense of orthodoxy he addressed

---

[4] *Columbian Centinel,* May 21, 1808.
[5] See Jedidiah Morse, *Sermon at the Ordination of Joshua Huntington,* Boston,
Mass.

Huntington as follows: "God in his providence is placing you, as a Watchman on a conspicuous part of the walls of his Jerusalem. It is at once a post of honor and of danger. Be ye therefore, humble, honest, vigilant and faithful; then fear not. They who will be for you, will be more than they who will be against you. Be steadfast, unmovable, always abounding in the work of the Lord, forasmuch as ye know that your labor is not in vain in the Lord. While you 'contend earnestly for the faith once delivered to the saints,' and are zealous for the truth, carefully cultivate a spirit of Christian charity, moderation and benevolence, and let your zeal be according to knowledge." [6]

But Morse had the habit of saying one thing in public while he was doing quite the opposite. As early as 1807, he and a small group of orthodox friends had become interested in establishing a strong church as a bulwark against liberalism in the heart of their opponents' territory—Boston. While in New York in the latter part of 1807, he was instructed by the Boston orthodox group to look for a suitable, prospective preacher to fill the pulpit of the proposed institution. Morse, consequently, approached his Presbyterian friend, Dr. Miller, but was unsuccessful in persuading him to separate from his church and come to Boston.[7] He then turned to Dr. Edward Dorr Griffin of Newark as a possibility, and secured the aid of Miller in urging Griffin to consider the matter. On the 24th of November, Miller wrote to Griffin thus:

Dr. Morse wishes me to converse with you. . . . Some worthy and influential gentlemen, devoted to the interests of evangelical truth, propose to build a large and handsome church in the heart of Boston, and to call one, if not two, able, evangelical and decided men to undertake the pastoral charge; and to make this, like the Seminary, a centre

[6] *Ibid.*
[7] For Miller's attitude, see pp. 134, 135, letter to John Codman.

of Orthodox operations. The persons concerned also wish to get a Pastor for this Church from the Southward. . . . Dr. Morse is much engaged on these subjects. He informs me that the funds of both institutions will be ample, and that discerning, pious people think they see in those institutions great and permanent benefit likely to redound to the interests of religion in Massachusetts and New England, and perhaps in the United States. He considers whoever is invited to take part in these institutions, as having a call not easily or lightly to be put aside. . . . The plan of establishing a new church in Boston is not at present ripe enough to be freely spoken of. Please consider it in confidence.

P. S. Dr. Morse earnestly wishes you to visit Charlestown and Boston as soon as possible.[8]

The following summer Griffin arranged the suggested visit, and preached in Massachusetts. The welcome he received proved that Morse had not misplaced his confidence. Communicating with Dwight, he wrote: "Mr. Griffin has made a very strong and universal impression this way in his favor. All the orthodox who are friends to our Institution and to Boston unite in saying,—'he must come.' " Even the Hopkinsians expressed an enthusiasm for Morse's selection. "Dr. S. [Spring] in a letter of yesterday among other things says —'you must write to Dr. Dwight, and tell him from us all that he must write to Gov. Strong and Mr. Griffin and compel them to accept.' . . . Pray use all your influence directly and through the clergy of New York to persuade Mr. Griffin to come over and help us. . . . Dr. S. [Spring] calls him the 'Mammoth Orator,' and adds that his people say 'that they never, never in their born days heard the like.' This indicates the impression made." [9]

That same summer, the brilliant preacher, Dr. Henry Kollock, a graduate of Princeton and pastor in Savannah,

[8] Sprague, *Life of Jedidiah Morse*, pp. 108, 109.
[9] Woods, *History of Andover Theological Seminary*, Letter, July 15, 1808. pp. 596, 597.

Georgia, visited Boston on his vacation and preached with "irresistible energy and power. Unaccustomed as we were," remarked one who heard Kollock preach, "to hear anything moving, his appeals came upon us like thunder. Crowds hung upon his lips, and confessed the power of earnest truth, earnestly preached." [10]

Seeing the enthusiasm with which Kollock was accepted, Morse was inspired to urge him to come to Boston and help in the establishment of the new church. Kollock indicated that he was favorable to the proposition and led Morse to believe that he would accept.

Thus assured of competent leadership for his new venture, the Charlestown pastor hastened to consummate the detailed arrangements, only to find himself confronted again by the Hopkinsian obstinacy. William Bartlet, their generous benefactor, was set on having Griffin as Professor of Pulpit Eloquence at Andover, and wished him to concentrate his efforts on that post alone. But Morse was no less determined to have the talents of Griffin serve his purpose at Boston. Consequently he set in motion, once again, the pressure of his dynamic personality and proposed to Griffin that he inform the Hopkinsians of his desire to occupy both the Andover position and the pulpit at Boston. To this suggestion Griffin replied in a letter to Morse: "I thank you particularly for the obliging sentiments contained in your letter. . . . Animated with such desires, and struggling with such difficulties to promote the interest of our common family, I feel that you are entitled to the generous thanks, and firm support of the whole Christian church. What I can consistently do with my feeble talents, and very limited influence, shall be done." However, he wished to be informed concerning the exact nature of the new church—"the principles on which a church is

[10] H. A. Hill: *History of the Old South Church*, II, 340.

to be formed . . . the importance of the object, all definitely explained. . . . Is the new church to be founded, and the sacraments to be administered on Edwardean principles ?" [11] Then he added his opinions as follows:

I am persuaded that the confidence, zeal and energies of the New England churches can never be enlisted . . . unless . . . the opinions of the revered Edwards "be favored." . . . The most evangelical, and therefore the most effective portion of the American churches, are I believe, every day becoming more and more impressed with the necessity of taking a decisive stand. Now I take it for granted that the Academy [Andover] and the new congregation will be generally understood to be united; and the public will look to the congregation for a practical illustration of the doctrine taught in the Academy. . . . May I add, that in my humble opinion, the immediate interest of the congregation itself greatly depends on preserving strictness in these matters. The stand to be made in Boston must be on ground encircled by a very distinct line of demarcation. Unless there be a visible and palpable difference between the old churches and the new ones, who will see any reason for coming over to the latter? Accessions will depend on accident and caprice rather than on principle, and who will rejoice in such accessions as additions to the Redeemer's Kingdom, or calculate on the permanency of ties so brittle and deceptive? In a congregation already formed and living in peace, good men will differ on the degree of indulgence to be exercised towards "tender consciences." But if there ever was a clear case for decision and thorough-going discipline, there is a call for both in the congregation to be formed, at this crisis in Boston. The motto which, glossed with "the meekness of wisdom," should be inscribed on the portals of the new church, and on the foreheads and hearts of the Pastors is this, "Come out from among them and be ye separate." Men of this decided character, if they are men of prayer and prudence, will succeed in Boston, and none else will, I believe.[12]

And he added to Morse, ". . . with perfect confidence in you, I commit the whole to your discretion." [13]

[11] Woods, *History of Andover Theological Seminary*, pp. 599–601.
[12] *Ibid.*, p. 601.
[13] *Ibid.*, Letter of July 28, 1808, from Newark, N. J., p. 602.

The result was that Griffin informed his wealthy sponsor, Bartlet, that he could not think of leaving Newark, either for Boston or for Andover; but that he might be willing to remove, "if he could, in some suitable way, be connected with both." To add to Morse's troubles with the Hopkinsians, Spring revealed a jealousy of Griffin. "I have had thoughts of holding my own in the pulpit, but if we do not confine the monster [Griffin] within the firm walls of the Institution, all will be up with poor me." [14] He also feared the man. "It is my real opinion that we shall raise him too high on the ladder to be safe, if we connect him with the Boston society. No man can stand long so high without being dizzy, or without being invidiously thrown down. I don't wish to see the mammoth fall." [15] And he added significantly, "I believe if I have heard right, that Dr. Griffin will not approve one of the peculiarities of the Boston connection. At any rate, if we do not mean to kill him, and wound the Institution, he must be confined to his professorship."

No doubt Spring feared that Griffin would not exhibit a strong Hopkinsian "consistency" in the new church, but knew that he could control him under the arrangement at Andover. Morse, again, was forced by circumstances to compromise with his chosen allies. The reviewer of Griffin's dedication sermon of the new church pointed out that "here as in another modern creed pretty well known" the Calvinistic doctrine of the imputation of Adam's sin is omitted. This was undoubtedly done in deference to the Hopkinsians, mainly to Spring their leader, and to Bartlet their benefactor. [16]

Here, as at Andover, Morse was the instrumentality in bringing a Presbyterian Calvinist and the "consistent Hop-

---

[14] *Ibid.*, Letter to Morse, July 15, 1808, pp. 595, 596.
[15] *Ibid.*, Letter of Spring to Morse, Oct. 6, 1808, p. 613.
[16] *Monthly Anthology*, Feb. 1810, VIII, 134.

kinsians" together for the sake of his espoused cause. It is evident that he diplomatically persuaded Griffin to come to Boston on the Hopkinsian terms. He knew that Bartlet and Spring would only coöperate on this basis. Spring wrote to Morse, "We at the north are all willing, and we wish to have it mutually understood at the outset, that Dr. Griffin shall spend much time in Boston, and do you and Boston friends more good, than can be possibly realized, in the plan of operation which you have proposed." [17] The following day he again wrote to Morse: "Pray if you must write soon to Dr. Griffin, press him to come on agreeably to Mr. Bartlet's communication. So it must be; and all will be well. But if we pursue any other plan we are undone. The path of consistency is the path of duty. If you will let us keep the road we shall enter the strong fortress; but if we leave the road and cross lots, we shall lose all, and plunge into inevitable evils." [18]

Griffin proved a stubborn man to win. But Morse, finally aided by his ally Leonard Woods, persuaded him to come to Andover and Boston on the Hopkinsian ground. Griffin confessed to Woods: "You are the hardest antagonist I ever had to encounter. There is something that you bring with you that one's heart cannot resist, and there is no way of breaking from you. And so I yield your willing captive." [19]

With this enthusiastic support promised, Morse and his friends proceeded to the final establishment of the new institution. From 1783 to 1810, Boston had grown in population from 18,000 to 33,000; it was felt that there was sufficient room for a new meeting-house. Bentley, however, remarked, "that from conversation with a candid minister of Boston, I

[17] Woods, *History of Andover Theological Seminary*, letter of Spring to Morse, Dec. 15, 1808, pp. 622, 623.

[18] *Ibid.*, Dec. 16, 1808, pp. 623–24.

[19] *Ibid.*, Letter, March 27, 1809, p. 629.

am informed that the overflowing of the Old South is a pretense. That a number of persons have purchased the site of the Old Granary at a heavy price and intend to erect a Meeting House for Kollock and Griffin." [20]

Several dissatisfied members of the Old South met, on February 27, 1809, with official delegates from the Charlestown, Cambridge, and Dorchester churches (the Federal Street and Old South churches were invited but declined to take part). This Council formed the new church. Morse preached the sermon from Psalms 118:25, "Save, now, I beseech thee; O Lord, O Lord, I beseech thee, send now prosperity." From the beginning, the church adopted a policy of exclusiveness. Terms of admission in the churches at Boston had been plain and simple; there was no requirement of assent to a definite system of divinity or a particular creed. The Park Street church, however, let it be known that it adhered to the doctrines of religion, as they are

in general clearly and happily expressed in the Westminister Shorter Catechism and in The Confession of Faith of 1680, but it formulated these doctrines in a symbol of its own, emphasizing expecially the tripersonality of the Godhead, election, (with its necessary corollary-reprobation) and imputed righteousness. And it went further; it required subscription both to the general statements and to its own particular confession, as a condition precedent to membership. It thus erected a barrier which would inevitably separate its minister, whoever he might be, from most of the ministers of the long-established churches, who were either negatively Calvinistic or positively Arminian. . . . Dr. Eckley, and his more conservative parishioners, must have foreseen that the gathering of a church with such a positive creed and in such an aggressive spirit, would add to the intensity of the doctrinal discussions then agitating the churches, and tend to promote a schism, which they would wish, if possible, to avert.[21]

[20] Bentley, *Diary*, III, 425.
[21] Hill, *History of the Old South Church*, II, 341, 342.

The cry immediately went up from liberal quarters that a schism was implied. "Bigotry, illiberality, exclusiveness; those old word-weapons were furbished up for the new war which had evidently opened, though not yet formally declared." [22] But Morse had anticipated this attitude and he was not downcast. Rather, he considered the establishment of the Park Street church "as marking an epoch in the religious history of New England," [23] and in truth it was. From this time on, the separation grew more marked.

Before the church had barely been organized, Kollock informed Morse that he would not accept the pastorate. Other men were sought, but without success. Finally, in desperation, Morse persuaded Griffin to give up his professorship at Andover and assume the full responsibility for the venture. Significantly enough, the Hopkinsian, Samuel Worcester of Salem, preached at the installation. Wrote Bentley: "Worcester ordained Griffin the emigrant from New Jersey, and Andover furnace at Boston, with all the exclusive hopes unassisted by the Association of the Capital and in open defiance of their judgment. . . . Griffin was hissed at Cambridge. . . ."[24] He has no concern with the Enlightened Clergy of that Capital and was inducted into his new charge by an Extraordinary Groupe, such as Morse of Charlestown, Holmes of Cambridge, Homer of Newton and Greenough of the same place assisted by Huntington of the Old South, Boston. I know all the men but the last and have no respect for their talents. But there is a kind of warfare with talents and the cause is properly supported." [25]

---

[22] Clark, *Historical Sketch of Congregational Churches in Massachusetts*, p. 235.

[23] Sprague, *Life of Jedidiah Morse*, p. 115.

[24] Bentley, *Diary*, IV, 54.

[25] *Ibid.*, p. 38. Griffin's ministry was not the success Morse had hoped it would be. After the war of 1812 he found it wise to return to his old pastorate in Newark. A letter in *The Spirit of the Pilgrims*, Vol. II, p. 221, states: "The

This experiment in "exclusiveness" so dramatically exhibited within the camp of the enemy was not without its effects in other parts of the state. An extensive corresponding change began to take place ". . . in the country. In many of the most important towns, the larger and more wealthy societies had come entirely under the same influences with those of Boston." [26] Morse was soon to find himself implicated in a significant controversy in the Second church in Dorchester, where orthodoxy again took the center of the stage for its exclusive rights. The pastor of the church was John Codman, an intimate friend of Morse's with whom he had been in the habit of exchanging pulpits.

Morse had "discovered" Codman for evangelical religion and his glorious cause in 1805. Codman had been trained theologically with Morse's liberal opponent, Henry Ware, and had been asked to write a review of Cooper's [27] sermons for the *Monthly Anthology*. However, it must have been with particular delight that Morse published the review as one of the "opening guns" of his *Panoplist* as a defense of orthodoxy, rather than a severe criticism of it.

To strengthen his new-found orthodox convictions Codman set out for a period of study at Edinburgh, equipped with letters of introduction from Morse. That his purpose was attained is evident in his reply to a letter that Morse wrote

church is deeply in debt, half of the pews are yet to let, and the good man himself [Griffin] by not returning the civilities paid him by the other ministers, when he first came to Boston, is now neglected, not only by them, but by their hearers; and he has to stand his ground, and plead the cause of Orthodoxy against eight of the Congregationalists, besides the King's Chapel minister."

Bentley later recorded in his *Diary* (iv, 327): Griffin's "boundless ambition proved vexatious even to the fanatic zeal of his patron Mr. Bartlet a merchant of Newburyport. . . . His light soon burnt into the socket and he now returns for the place from whence he came. He has observed a rigid separation from the churches in Boston who were not of the first zeal."

[26] E. C. Tracy, *Memoir of Jeremiah Evarts*, pp. 60, 61.

[27] *Ibid.*, p. 25. The Rev. William Cooper was minister of the Brattle Street Church, Boston.

from Charlestown. "You observe," he stated, "that Harvard College is yet destitute of a President. Whoever he may be, I pray God he may have right views of the blessed gospel. I am sorry to hear of the publication of Mr. W. Sherman's vindication of Arianism. It appears to me, my dear Sir, that greater anti-christs than the Pope of Rome, are rising in the world. 'He is anti-christ that denieth the Father and the Son.' . . . I unite with you in the prayer that the great Head of the church would overrule all these things for the advancement of his kingdom." [28]

Shortly after his return to America the newly formed Dorchester church invited Codman to become its pastor. Bentley claimed that the people of the church "considered his wealth and opportunities and not his talents and opinions." [29] Apparently a number of the liberal-minded overlooked his avowed orthodoxy on the assumption that he would be charitable toward those of their opinion because of his early liberal environment, his friendship and contacts with the Liberals, and because of the social position maintained by his wealth.

In a letter to the congregation, Codman made clear his sentiments before accepting the call:

I think it my duty in the presence of a heart-searching God, and of this church, to declare my firm, unshaken faith in those doctrines that are sometimes called the doctrines of the reformation, the doctrine of the cross, the peculiar doctrines of the gospel. These doctrines through the help of God, I intend to preach; in the faith of these doctrines, I hope to live; and in the faith of these doctrines, I hope to die. . . . As Arian and Socinian errors have of late years crept into some of our churches, I think it my duty to declare to that Church of Christ, of whom I may have the pastoral charge, that I believe the Father, Son and Holy Ghost, to be the one living and true God, and that my faith, in general, is conformable to the Assembly's Catechism. . . .[30]

[28] Yale Letter, Jan. 7, 1806.
[29] Bentley, *Diary*, IV, 64.
[30] William Allen, *Memoir of John Codman*, p. 70.

133

Morse was one of the ordaining council that met and approved of Codman on December 7, 1808. Mr. Channing preached the ordination sermon.

Codman had not labored long in his new position when it was seen that his convictions led him to refuse to exchange pulpits with certain liberals with whom he disagreed. A number of the socially prominent and wealthy people in the parish expressed disappointment "from your not making your exchanges generally, with those ministers who preach the public lectures in Boston, on Thursday, and with them indiscriminately." [31] "We could not withhold our protest," it was later remarked, "against a system, calculated in effect to make us a separate religious society; cutting us off from that intercourse with the greater part of the Christian societies of our own denomination, by which our friendship and communion with them had been preserved." [32]

But Codman stood his ground confidently. His attitude was strengthened and supported by encouragement from many of his orthodox friends, including the strong Hopkinsian, Dr. Samuel Worcester of Salem.[33] Dr. Miller, the prominent Presbyterian of New York whom Morse had tried to secure as preacher for his Park Street church, wrote to Codman stating: "I hope and believe, my dear brother, from what I hear, that you are determined whatever may occur, to adhere to

[31] Dorchester, Mass., *Memorial of the Proprietors of the New South Meeting House*, 1813, p. 40.

[32] *Ibid.*, p. 46.

[33] "In the Dorchester Controversy, he [Worcester], had a leading part, as the friend and counsellor of the late Dr. Codman." (*Life and Labors of Rev. Samuel Worcester, D.D.*, Vol. II, by Samuel M. Worcester, his son, p. 217.)
It was in the private sessions of the Council, "that Dr. Worcester's greatest power was exerted. . . . While he was speaking, he (Mr. Evarts) was so much overpowered with satisfaction and admiration, that, every few minutes, he would turn to the delegate of the Tabernacle Church, who sat near, and as loud as decorum would permit, he whispered his exclamations, 'Admirable! Admirable! It is a better argument than Dexter's; it is ABSOLUTELY CONCLUSIVE!'" Worcester, *Life and Labors*, p. 219.

your original resolution respecting exchanges with ministers of heterodox or doubtful sentiments. I am as firmly persuaded that it is your duty to do so. . . . No minister, situated as you are, can possibly recede from the ground you have taken, without yielding a most important advantage to the enemy, and without inflicting a deep and lasting injury on the cause of truth.[34]. . . I am more and more convinced that the friends of evangelical truth in Boston and its neighborhood must consent, at least for a time, to be a little and comparatively a despised flock. They must form a little world of their own, and patiently bear all the ridicule and insults of their proud and wealthy foes. When [though] all the wit, and learning and wealth and power of the world were leagued against them, they will . . . certainly finally triumph over the enemies of Christ." [35]

Morse sympathized with his friend in the controversy but realized that such action might result in dividing the historic Congregational fellowship. It was his constant hope that through the efforts of the Orthodox, "pure and undefiled religion" would return to all the churches and that unity would be maintained. Consequently when he received a request from the dissatisfied Dorchester group to refuse to exchange with Codman, he replied: "Your communication is of so extraordinary and unprecedented a nature, that I have really been at a loss to know how to notice it, or in what manner to conduct in reference to the very singular request which it contains. . . . I cannot but think you will at once perceive its impropriety, inconsistency, and direct tendency to excite divisions, and to subvert all ecclesiastical order." [36]

The situation in Morse's church was such that he could not

---

[34] Allen, *Memoir of John Codman*, p. 101.
[35] *Ibid.*, pp. 106–7.
[36] Dorchester, Mass., *Proceedings of the Second Church*, 1812, pp. 40–42.

afford to draw the line too exclusively. In a note to Lathrop, he wrote: "If such a principle [of depriving a minister of his church on his refusal to exchange indiscriminately] were admitted as correct, there is not a faithful minister in this whole region, holding the doctrines which you hold . . . who would be permitted long to remain in his station. In every parish there would be found a sufficient number (at least as many as existed originally in the Dorchester Society, which did not exceed three or four), on this principle to remove him." [37]

In this period of the Dorchester controversy, Morse was chosen to deliver the Annual Convention sermon before the Congregational ministers assembled at Boston. His plea was for "unity in love." "The universal and effectual cure for all errors in religion, and for all theological controversies and unchristian contention among the professed disciples of Christ," he stated, was in his text; "Now the end of the commandment is charity, out of a pure heart, and of a good conscience, and of faith unfeigned." [38] "Our subject leads us to the important discovery of a simple, easy, and happy method, by which all our calamitous divisions, both in church and state, may be effectually healed, and a final end be put to all our political and religious controversies. Let us but possess true charity in our hearts, and exhibit its kindly fruits in our conversation and lives, and the whole business is accomplished." [39] But his interpretation of the uniting principle of charity resolved itself practically into the acceptance of a creed, in defense of which Morse felt it one's duty to "sacrifice his life." [40] Undoubtedly he was sincere in this expression, but because of his close association with the Hopkinsians he

---

[37] Sprague, *Life of Jedidiah Morse*, p. 119.
[38] Jedidiah Morse, *Convention Sermon*, 1812, p. 7.
[39] *Ibid.*, pp. 22, 23.
[40] *Ibid.*, p. 21.

found that he could not apply such sentiments to his active relationships with his liberal friends. Intellectually and socially, he longed for "unity in charity," but, forced by necessity into a coalition with the strict Hopkinsians, he could not shake off their "exclusiveness." It was this contradictory aspect of Morse's life that aroused the scorn and contempt of his antagonists and eventually proved his ultimate ruin.[41]

In council and correspondence, Morse consequently supported Codman's position. Woods communicated with Morse: "I rejoice to hear that Mr. Codman looks up and stands forth. The Lord be with him. The devil is quite angry as I suspect and cannot sleep. He is terribly beat, by rich and poor—I guess his own rich ones won't do all he wishes with their money." [42]

Jeremiah Evarts, Morse's intimate friend and publisher of the *Panoplist,* also influenced by his contacts with Hopkinsian friends, wrote a lengthy review of the Dorchester controversy and published it in his *Magazine* [43] (*Panoplist*) (1814). Morse and Evarts had attended the Dorchester council together as delegates from the Charlestown church and were familiar with the situation. Defending the publication of the review, Evarts wrote:

The ostensible and real causes of this controversy are of general and permanent importance, and ought to excite a correspondent degree of interest. . . . Mr. Codman had not labored many months among

[41] From his perspective of England, Wilberforce sensed this condition. He wrote to Morse: "Your accounts of the religious state of your country are peculiarly interesting. Excuse my saying that there are some circumstances, both in your political and your ecclesiastical condition, that appear to me, if not actually to favor the progress of Socinianism; yet to make it right—to guard against it with jealous circumspection. I rejoice, therefore, to see that it is opposed so zealously. May the blessing of God prosper your holy warfare, justly to be so termed." (Letter of W. Wilberforce to Morse, Sept. 9, 1815; in New York Public Library Collection.)

[42] Yale Letter, March 23, 1809.

[43] For Evart's attitude, see p. 142, note 57.

his people before it was found, that the preaching of those doctrines, which he had all along professed and inculcated, gave serious offense to a part of his hearers, who soon began to form and organize a regular opposition. That this opposition originated, in fact, from a dislike of the great truths which Mr. Codman preached, and the correspondent strictness of moral deportment which he urged, we have the fullest persuasion; and we think no candid man, having an intimate acquaintance with the parties and the controversy, can entertain a doubt on the subject. Had Mr. C. delivered smooth harangues on the native benevolence and dignity of man; complimented his people, occasionally, on their candor, catholicism, and liberality; inveighed earnestly, and with a very significant air and tone, against creeds, intolerance, bigotry, and enthusiasm, and countenanced such innocent amusements, as playing at cards, and midnight revelling, it is altogether possible that he would have remained unmolested by those who took a lead in the controversy with him, and that the question of ministerial exchanges would have been suffered by them to sleep in silence.[44]

Joshua Bates,[45] who likewise received a letter, as had Morse, from the opposing Dorchester group recalled that "that portion of his [Codman's] parish who commenced the opposition were a gay people, exceedingly fond of amusements; and there can be no doubt, that they determined to oppose everything which interfered with their favorite indulgences. . . . Hence, they began to complain of his preaching so much on human depravity, the guilt and consequences of sin, the doc-

[44] Review in *Panoplist*, 1814, pp. 3, 7.

[45] Dr. Joshua Bates, also concerned in the controversy, coincided with Evarts in his opinion: "To us it was perfectly evident that the pungent preaching, the full and clear exhibition of the humbling doctrines of the gospel, with the practical bearing always given to them, and the application of them to the hearts and consciences of the hearers, was the first great moving cause of the opposition. It was manifest that this was the exciting cause, because the first complaints made against Mr. Codman were confined to this subject. These complaints, whether made directly to him or others about him, all had reference to his preaching; and especially to its directness and forcible application. . . . Mr. Codman's preaching was peculiarly pungent, and his applications generally direct; and what rendered his preaching more offensive at that time, and in that region, was, that his practise was consistent with it, and therefore full of rebuke and admonition." (Allen, *Memoir of John Codman*, pp. 187, 188.)

trine of the atonement, and the necessity of faith, repentance and regeneration." [46]

The Dorchester liberals denied this. "We wish it to be distinctly understood, that a dissatisfaction with the doctrines, which Mr. Codman has preached, or a difference in religious sentiments, has constituted no part of our complaint against him." [47] However, their original letter to Codman insinuated a different attitude.[48] There was a strong indication that the arising tension in the established churches had its root at this point. Those who had attained some measure of wealth and cultivation in each community were growing more and more irritated by the constant emphasis of the orthodox preachers on the peculiarities of the strict, "consistent" Hopkinsianism. The churches in which these members of liberal sentiments found their preacher offering tirades of Calvinistic doctrines soon began to grow restless. While this growing uneasiness put the orthodox on the defensive it also led them to demand "true righteousness" more vociferously. The parishes in which liberal ministers were settled, and where there was a preponderance of the cultured and wealthy, slipped silently and without controversy into the latitudinarian attitude.

Morse fought a strenuous battle in the midst of the Liberals. He inadvertently hastened the climax by choosing to associate himself more exclusively with the Hopkinsians. "Last week," wrote Bentley in July, 1811, "for the first time, the New Association of Salem, called the Union, met in Salem. It is said to embrace the ministers of that Society. . . . It is said Dr. Morse is to join it and to leave the Boston Association. So the Inflammatory party intend to get strength in Essex. The Boston Association are firm against the projects of this

[46] Allen, *Memoir of John Codman*, p. 189.
[47] *Memorial of Proprietors of New South Meeting House in Dorchester, Massachusetts*, p. 46.
[48] *Ibid.*, pp. 39–40.

party. . . . The alarm is so great among the feeble that Witchcraft was never more powerful upon the imaginations of 1692. And this is the time to give success to the friends of superstition in our Country. The illuminati tales are not told but combinations are hinted at as formed already against Christianity." [49]

The Hopkinsian doctrines gave the Liberals a clear-cut theology to attack and they lost no opportunity to do so. The *Monthly Anthology* had been replaced by the more militant and controversial *General Repository* as the voice of the Liberals. Consequently, when Ezra Stiles Ely, stated preacher in the Hospital and Almshouse in the city of New York, published his *Contrast between Calvinism and Hopkinsianism* (1811), the *General Repository* seized it as a lever to expose the Orthodox. The reviewer was the Reverend Mr. Holley of Boston. He was unsparing in his attack on the combination of Hopkinsians and Calvinists at Andover, which Morse had maneuvered. He claimed they "have deluded themselves . . . by their reiterated and exclusive pretensions to orthodoxy and evangelical purity."

This *Contrast* served as one of the contributing causes of the final separation in the churches. Referring to the "Hopkinsians, Andoverians, or New England Calvinists," Holley wrote that

you are to be known; a line of distinction is to be drawn against you; . . . you are to be exposed immediately, and reprobated in the most decided manner; you are afraid of the light, preaching another gospel; you have revived the old Gnostic heresy of being in general, of abstract beauty, of disinterested love, and the best of all possible worlds; your philosophy is contemptible; your consequences from your premises are shocking and impious; you speak with a familiar and disgusting irreverence of the Most High; you are not only guilty of nonsense and

[49] Bentley, *Diary*, IV, 33, 34.

impiety, but you render Christianity itself incredible and detestable;
you are the fathers of future infidelity and atheism; and though you
should come in the form of angels from heaven you must be denounced and resisted! [50]

Here was a battle cry from the other side. Slowly the
liberals seemed to awaken to a championship of their cause.
They now were more secure in what they had to denounce.
"Andoverian Calvinism is, without a question, not Presbyterian Calvinism, and, with as little doubt, it is . . . Hopkinsianism" [51] "The plain English is, Andoverians, we know
you, stand off, or be converted from your errors." [52] Holley
continued with his liberal observations. Andover "is under
the decided management of Hopkinsian policy. The middle-
ground men have either become cold toward it, or have floated
with the popular tide." [53] The *Panoplist* "is the adopted
child of the Hopkinsians or Andoverian Calvinists; and, has
been the means of circulating misrepresentations, and exciting much prejudice against catholic Christians, particularly
those in the neighborhood of Boston." [54]

The attack of Drs. Morse, Spring and others, upon Harvard University, respecting the election of the Hollis Professor of theology, has
given an activity to catholic Christians, which will long produce valuable consequences. . . . In many, if not in most instances, where a
change from a catholic mode of preaching to the exclusive and de-
nouncing spirit of Andoverian Calvinism has taken place, contentions,
divisions, and the multiplication of checks have followed. . . . The
violence and denunciations of Andoverian Calvinists in the metropolis
have shown the people the value of catholicism and of their religious
liberties; have taught them the deformity of sectarism; have enlarged
and emancipated many minds from the prejudices which were grow-

---

[50] *General Repository*, 1813, II, 341.
[51] *Ibid.*, p. 350.
[52] *Ibid.*, p. 356.
[53] *Ibid.*, p. 359.
[54] *Ibid.*, 369.

ing upon them; and have given full proof that the project, to revolutionize the town from genuine protestantism to the sentiments and dominion of Andover, must not only fail now, but can never be successful.[55]

And finally he adds, "Let the truth be brought before the public, and they cannot fail to see, embrace, and follow it. Our laymen . . . are fast discovering that infidelity is the product of religious abuses, and that real Christianity is simple, practicable, reasonable, divine, and full of the most noble principles, affections, and hopes." [56]

This article is illustrative of the rapid progress of the controversy. Only a few years previous to this, Morse had given the closing prayer at Holley's installation as pastor of the Hollis Street church in Boston.[57]

[55] *Ibid.*, p. 372.

[56] *Ibid.*, p. 369.

[57] At a later date, Morse and the orthodox had occasion to retaliate against Holley. When Holley was being considered for the position of presidency of Transylvania College, in Kentucky, inquiries came to Morse concerning the candidate's sentiments. Morse replied (Dec. 12, 1815: "His [Holley's] religious opinions are very wide from what is called the orthodox faith . . . but are what are called peculiar doctrines of the gospel. . . . He openly impugns the Westminister Confession and the Apostles catechism. . . . He is considered by the Unitarian clergy of Boston as well as by the orthodox . . . as a Unitarian or Socinian of the lowest class, but a grade above infidelity, as ranking in point of religious opinions with such men as Bentley, Lindsey, Wakefield and Belsham. . . . He was orthodox when in Greenfield, Conn., but has changed his faith and now, as the orthodox believe, preaches another gospel." (Yale Letter, Dec. 12, 1815, to Luther Rice.)

Jeremiah Evarts supported Morse in this conviction. He wrote to Rice the following day, Dec. 13, 1815: "I entirely approve of what he [Dr. Morse] has written [on Holley's religious opinions], and am perfectly willing to add, that all the orthodox in this region consider Mr. Holley as differing very little, if at all, from an open infidel, and that during the progress of the late Unitarian controversy here, nobody of any party has ever hinted that Mr. Holley is injured by being ranked with Mr. Belsham, who holds that our Saviour was an 'ignorant, fallible, peccable man.' " (Letter in N. Y. Public Library collection, Dec. 13, 1815.)

Morse's retaliation had its effect as indicated in a letter he received from Rice, Nov. 24, 1817. "The long contested election of the Rev. Mr. Holley of Boston—your neighbor—for the presidential chair in the Transylvania university, took place on the 15th inst. It is with real regret to all the religious people in this Town—and especially to such of them, as are denominated Calvinists—that this

The effect of Ely's *Contrast* was immediately felt. One pastor wrote, "By classing Hopkinsianism, Arminianism, and other 'isms,' in the ranks of Heresy, you have thrown the Gauntlet and invited to a combat on controversial ground. By adducing Calvinism as the true test of christian doctrines, you have given your opponents a decided advantage over you; as they must all consider the Holy Scriptures to be the only true test—and your substitution of Calvinism therefore, is an unequivocal, and very unhappy departure from orthodox christianity." [58]

As the tension grew between the two parties, Morse tried to rid himself, once and for all, of the handicap placed upon him by the Hannah Adams charge. His son consented to aid him in gathering the documents in reference to the long conflict and they were published at this time.[59] The result was not

---

election was ever made. . . . All who know anything of his character know that he is a thorough-faced Socinian or Unitarian. The religious people of this country are trinitarians—except an obscure corner of ignorant Baptists and the dregs of those enthusiasts, who dissented from the Churches in this country, during the revival in 1801–2—I am well assured—nay I am morally certain should Mr. Holley accept the appointment the religious people of this country will array themselves against him, and the growing state of our University must and will decline as it did under the presidency of the Socinian Toleman." (Yale Letter, Nov. 24, 1817.)

[58] James Wilson, *Letters to the Rev. Ezra Stiles Ely*, p. 5. James Wilson was pastor of the Second Congregational Church in Providence, Rhode Island.

[59] There is an indication that Morse may have been led to emphasize the religious implications of his personal controversy by the urgency of getting it before the public at large. He wrote to several of his friends asking their opinion of printing his *Appeal* in the *Panoplist*. From Enoch Hale, of Westhampton, he received the reply: "If the review be so written that the readers, with the prepossession against which I believe they naturally have, see that the controversy is about religion and not property, nor any personal consideration, the effect I think may be beneficial." (Letter in N. Y. Public Library, March 1, 1815.)

The same inquiry of Dr. J. Lyman brought the following comments: "The great difficulty of a review seemed to be the impracticability of making the public in general sensible that the controversy was not mainly personal; that it immediately concerned the public and the cause of evangelical truth. . . . But if the writer could be morally certain that conviction could be assured to the public mind that the controversy was not personal but that the Christian public were intimately affected by the controversy and truth was concerned in a development

all that Morse expected. Upon hearing of the document William Bentley poured out his scorn for the Charlestown divine upon the pages of his *Diary*, concluding, "His hand is against every man. It is time he was fully known." [60]

Furthermore, when Morse sought to exchange pulpits with his friends, he often found the liberal element objected strenuously to having him appear in their pulpits. Dr. Joseph Lathrop wrote that

your worthy deacon called in your name to propose an exchange of pulpits, on the Lord's morn. Having informed him that Mr. Evarts had engaged to preach for me, we entered into conversation on the supposed and perhaps real differences of opinion between you and the minister of Boston and (perhaps) generally of the Association of Boston and the vicinity; and on the same topic of a particular kind, which have occupied unpleasant feelings among some in most of our congregations, relating to yourself. I told the deacon, that some of my church and some very influential members, had signified to me it would be unpleasant, under exciting circumstances, to have exchanges take place between us as heretofore. . . . It was his [Morse's deacon's] opinion that a suspension of exchanges for a time might be prudent.[61]

Consequently, chafing under this personal dishonor, and struggling on losing ground, Morse made one more desperate effort to expose his opponents. This time its effectiveness must have startled the author himself. Samuel Finley Breese, his oldest son, was studying art in England and learned that Thomas Belsham's *Memoirs of the Life of Theophilus Lindsey*, published in London, contained an account of Unitarianism in the United States. He communicated this discovery to his father who immediately set out to secure a copy of the book. The one copy in the Harvard library was not

---

of the dispute, then it might do good. . . ." (Letter in N. Y. Public Library, March 17, 1815.)

[60] Bentley, *Diary*, IV, 241–42.

[61] Letter in N. Y. Public Library, from Boston, March 27, 1815.

available because of its constant use. Morse experienced great difficulty in securing the *Memoir*. "It is a fact," stated a later review in the Boston *Patriot*, "that the work no sooner arrived here, than it was studiously concealed. . . . On a careful perusual, we can find but one motive for this suppression, viz; that the Unitarians, who are principally confined to Boston and its vicinity, are not yet prepared for an open and explicit avowal of their sentiments." [62]

Finally Morse obtained a copy from a friend in Boston and read with eagerness that for which he had long been looking—a definite proof, in black and white, of the avowed Unitarian sentiment. He immediately financed a private publication of the portion of the book referring to the American churches, prefacing it with the statement:

When such radical and essential changes take place in the religion of a country, as have been witnessed in some parts of New England, particularly in Boston and in the region round about it, during the last thirty years, it is gratifying to inquiring minds to know, from correct and undisputed sources and documents, in what manner and by what steps such changes have been effected. The publishers of this pamphlet are happy that they have it in their power to satisfy the inquisitive on this subject. . . . We mean here to offer no opinion of our own; to introduce nothing of controversy, but mainly to give a plain history of very important facts, derived from unquestionable sources, disclosing the instruments and operations by which these great and visible changes in the religious faith of so many of our Clergy, of the Churches, and of the University in this part of New England, have been accomplished. [63]

Along with the personal letters of James Freeman, William Wells,[64] and others, Morse included the religious creed of Mr. Belsham.

[62] *Boston Patriot*, May 13, 1815.
[63] Jedidiah Morse, *American Unitarianism*, pp. 1, 3, and 4.
[64] "Before I came to this country (1793) I wrote to Dr. Morse, respecting a removal hither; informing him I was no great stickler for particular sentiments

Morse evidently felt that it was wise for him not to carry the brunt of this attack entirely upon his own shoulders. The situation in his church was growing more critical and he was anxious to spare himself more personal grief such as the Hannah Adams difficulty. The result was that while he remained in the background he persuaded others to take up the standard. His friend, Jeremiah Evarts, consented to write a review of his pamphlet for publication in the *Panoplist*. The fact that the review was attributed to the pen of Morse indicates that these two orthodox leaders no doubt collaborated in its composition. The startling review made its appearance in the June, 1815, issue. "We regard," it stated, "the appearance of this pamphlet as one of the most important events, which have taken place for many years, in reference to the interest of religion in our country." [65] The review continued with an emphasis upon three points: the identity of the American liberals with the English Unitarians, the dishonesty of their attempt to conceal their opinions, and a plea for separation. On the last point it stated significantly, "Let the orthodox come out and be separate . . . in worship and communion from Unitarians; but let them meekly give a reason for their separation." [66] It dramatically concluded: "We have heard 'the dull hollow rumbling at the bottom of the Sea.' We exhort the churches 'to listen to the friendly premonition': lest, when the fountains of the great deep shall be

---

in religion; being well assured that many wiser and better than myself differed from me both on the one side and on the other. But as it was generally reckoned there should be some considerable agreement between a minister and his people, I would observe, I might perhaps be justly styled a moderate Baxterian, there being no other I was acquainted with, who more generally agreed with me on religious subjects than he did. The Dr. answered, there were many ministers in New England of similar sentiments with mine." (*Some Observations Taken in Part from an Address Delivered in the New Meeting House in Brattleborough*, July 7, 1816, p. 2.)

[65] *Panoplist*, 1815, p. 1.
[66] *Ibid.*, p. 26.

broken up, those who are careless and inattentive should be overwhelmed by 'the imprisoned waves' to 'their consternation and utter destruction.' " [67] It would be mild to say that the pamphlet and review excited great interest. Coming at the close of the war with England, it created almost as much concern as that event in New England. Within five months, five editions were sold out. Men such as John Adams were inspired to comment upon the subject.[68]

The Liberals were thoroughly aroused. Thacher, the reviewer of the Andover creed, set out to pen a reply, but wisely turned the task over to his more cautious friend, W. E. Channing of the Federal St. Church, Boston. The liberal reply accordingly appeared several weeks later as a "Letter to Rev. Samuel C. Thacher, on the Aspersions contained in a late number of the *Panoplist*, on the Ministers of Boston and the Vicinity" by Channing.

The battle was finally breaking on open ground, but the avowed leader of the orthodox saw fit to withdraw in favor of others. The Unitarian pamphlet had been his culminating attack by which he felt he achieved part of his life purpose of "preserving the faith once delivered to the saints" in exposing its hidden enemies. The by-product of separation he reluctantly accepted as one of the inevitable consequences. He wrote to his son Samuel Finley Breese: "A pretty warm religious controversy is now on the carpet in which Mr. Channing has come out the champion of the Unitarian side. Dr. Worcester of Salem has answered him. The future course of things in relation to this controversy cannot be foreseen. I wish that it may be conducted with a Christian spirit on both sides, and issue in favor of the cause of truth. I believe the Trinitarians and Unitarians will, after this, be separate, as

[67] *Ibid.*, p. 31.
[68] Sprague, *Life of Jedidiah Morse*, pp. 125, 126.

they now are in England. The points of difference between them are such, as they can never agree. I hope they may agree kindly to differ. . . ." [69]

In spite of the fact that Morse relinquished the leadership of the struggle to his Hopkinsian ally, Dr. Samuel Worcester, he still suffered from the criticisms of his opponents. John Lowell, a layman, published, anonymously, a pamphlet entitled, "Are You a Christian or a Calvinist?," in which he directly denounced Morse along with Worcester in such phrases as: "Is it then, because Dr. Morse and Dr. Worcester know more of the character of God and of our Saviour, than Jesus Christ knew of himself, that we are called upon to believe this incomprehensible doctrine, and to reject and view with abhorrence those venerable pastors, who prefer the authority of Christ to that of these fallible mortals?" [70] "You have had all the learning which Professor Stewart could infuse into you, you have all the grace and goodness and unction which Dr. Morse could communicate. . . ." [71] I am ready to acknowledge that any doctrine which would compel me to believe that Dr. Morse was a saint and Mr. Channing a sinner, that the first was acceptable to God, while the other was the object of his wrath, that the former was the friend of Jesus and the latter his foe, I should for that reason ALONE reject. I should do it on just grounds. For I should say, 'my reason may be fallible, arguments may deceive me, but experience cannot.' . . . I say therefore, Dr. Morse may be a better Calvinist. He might perhaps contend more zealously, and be more ready to burn Mr. Thacher as his master did Servetus, but I doubt whether he is a better christian;

[69] Yale Letter, July 19, 1815.
[70] John Lowell, *Are You a Christian or a Calvinist?*, p. 7.
[71] *Ibid.*, p. 14.

that is I doubt whether he has a greater love for Christ, or is more disposed to obey his precepts." [72]

The pamphlet made the concluding remarks:

We cannot review the state of religious controversy in Mass. and the recent clamours which have been excited against certain pastors and certain tenets, without recollecting, what we know to be the fact, that for many years, Dr. Morse, and those who have chosen to identify their cause with his character and views, knew as well as they now do, that many of the Boston clergy held opinions opposed to those of Calvin, and in conformity with the simple doctrines which our Saviour himself taught. They knew also, that these opinions were generally prevalent among the laity in their parishes. Yet, during all this period, Dr. Morse courted their friendship, and held an intimate intercourse with the men he now denounces as heretical. It was not till after his ambitious views on the college were defeated, and till most of the parishes in Boston felt a repugnance to his introduction into their pulpits, on various grounds, that he became an open assailant.[73]

Indeed, the bitter fruit of the controversy began to be gathered in his own church at Charlestown. The rumbling undercurrents, long existent, broke out on the surface, and Morse, leaving his position of leadership to the Hopkinsians, turned his thoughts to his local parish.

[72] *Ibid.*, p. 19.
[73] *Ibid.*, p. 61.

CHAPTER X

RETREAT FROM CHARLESTOWN

AT AN early period in Morse's ministry at Charlestown he had encountered dissatisfaction among some of his own parishioners. In 1796 he threatened to resign when conditions were such that he did not receive his full salary. Commenting upon the situation Morse wrote:

I have no reason to doubt the sincere attachment of my numerous Church, nor the friendship of all the most wealthy and respectable part of the rest of the congregation. I have often received from all of them the most unequivocal marks of respect and esteem. Yet those who appear united in me, seem so disunited among themselves, through various unfortunate circumstances, that it seems to me impossible they will ever be able to devise or execute, unitedly, any plan which will remove the existing obstacles to my continuance here.[1]

The existing arrangement whereby "all the legal voters of the town had a right to attend parish-meetings, and to vote on all matters that came before that Body" gave the dissatisfied an opportunity to register their disapproval of the minister. The population of Charlestown had greatly increased by immigration since the Revolution. The economic prosperity of the state was equally felt in this town as elsewhere. "The community was active and intelligent. Differing beliefs in politics and in religion had grown with the institution of the young republic, and these last were showing their effect upon the various divisions of the people." [2] Morse found the pew-

[1] W. B. Sprague, *Life of Jedidiah Morse*, p. 34.
[2] J. F. Hunnewell, *Historical Sketch of Charlestown*, p. 41.

holders in his church outvoted by this newer element in town on matters relative to his salary and to intimate concerns of his parish. Consequently, he managed, in spite of vigorous opposition, to secure an Act incorporating the church.

For a while all was quiet, until complaints arose from church members that Morse was spending too much time on his geographical works and not paying enough attention to the duties of his parish. There is an indication that this was made an excuse for objection to Morse on other grounds. Writing to his Parish Committee on January 7, 1804, Morse stated:

There are men whose influence and respectability and standing in the church render their opposition weighty and worthy of serious regard of a church minister; who absolutely, and as they say, conscientiously refuse to pay their proportion of my stipulated support unless compelled by law. And for a minister of peace, whose usefulness so essentially depends on his enjoying the . . . confidence of his people to submit to receive a support which shall have been thus drawn from his parishioners and even from wealthy and influential members of his church by force of law, would subject both minister and such individuals to such reproach and disgrace as would reflect greatly on honor and religion.[3]

About 1810, some of the newer element in the population and many of the younger generation welcomed the establishment of the First Universalist Church in Charlestown. Even some of the older residents such as the "Frothinghams, Harrises, Rand's, and Woods" were interested, and the new society "had enterprise and a fair degree of wealth." [4] Still there was a growing dissatisfaction with Morse. Deacon Warren wrote to him in 1814 "urging him to be more concerned with his parish duties than to public controversies." Morse recognized not only this opposition and discontent but the increasing in-

[3] Charlestown Church papers, Congregational Library, Boston.
[4] Hunnewell, *Sketch of Charlestown*, pp. 25, 26.

difference to his evangelical preaching. "For the last ten months," he addressed his parishioners, "there have been no additions to this church; so long an interval of the kind has not before occurred since my settlement with you." [5] He had been hearing of the great revivals to the south, no doubt, with jealousy. His Presbyterian friend, Ashbel Green, wrote; "There is a glorious revival at Princeton." And referring to the similar movement at Yale, "it appears that there is a wonderful similarity between what is taking place at Yale and what was witnessed here in January." [6] It was with no little disappointment and deep grief that Morse's efforts to revive the evangelical sentiments of his Charlestown flock fell upon cold hearts.

Desperately he tried to summon his people to respond to their duty. In July, 1816, he pleaded with them: "Some who dwell among us, though often admonished of their sins, have absented themselves month after month, and year after year, from our Communion and worship. Others have been left to fall into open immoralities, for which, though reproved privately, and in some instances publicly, they have not been brought to repentance and reformation, and still remain in their sins, and in connection with the Church." [7] To follow up this appeal, he proposed a church day of fasting, humiliation, and prayer, the disciplining of delinquent members and the appointment of a "discreet" committee to investigate "the particular condition of all the individuals whose names stand on the records of the Church as members." [8]

This was more than the disaffected group could stand. It was the final act which inspired a break in Morse's fellowship. And to cap the climax Morse proceeded to break his

[5] Sprague, *Life of Jedidiah Morse*, p. 40.
[6] Letter, April 12, 1815, in N. Y. Public Library.
[7] Sprague, *Life of J. Morse*, p. 40.
[8] *Ibid.*, pp. 40, 41.

custom of exchanging pulpits with his former liberal friends. After Codman's stand and the review of the Unitarian pamphlet in the *Panoplist*, there was nothing left for Morse to do but assert his exclusiveness and break relations with those "in error." [9] Those dissatisfied with Morse were a minority and deemed it wise to withdraw quietly and organize a church in which they could hear a minister of their own sentiments. "The peace with England," wrote Dr. Walker, "which took place about this time had something to do with the gathering of this church. That event, it will be recollected, had the effect to produce a general amnesty in regard to political differences; so that nothing was left of the estrangements originating in political causes to hinder those who thought and felt alike on the subject of religion from coming together, and acting in concert." [10]

At the same time, the Baptist meeting house on High street passed to the estate of Mr. James Harrison, "then recently deceased, and was offered for sale by his executor. This circumstance was opportune, and the disaffected minority . . . lost no time in availing of it." [11] Previously, several of Morse's congregation [12] had purchased pews in the Baptist church, though they were "not in accord with the peculiar doctrines of the Baptist Communion, but attended regularly the preaching of their several ministers in preference to listen-

---

[9] "Most of the clergymen in the central and eastern parts of the state depended much, if not chiefly, on those who were of different sentiments from themselves, for hearers and for support; who continued to hear and support from personal regard to their ministers; while they (Ministers) continued to give them an opportunity for hearing men of their own views by way of exchange. When the privilege, or right as they would regard it, was denied them, there was a shock, which was deeply felt by minister, as well as people, and a fountain of bitter waters was opened. . . ." (Samuel Willard, *Historical Sermon at Deerfield*, Sept. 22, 1858, p. 31.)

[10] Henry H. Edes, *History of Harvard Church*, p. 55.

[11] *Ibid.*, pp. 81, 82.

[12] David Devens, Nathaniel Austin, Sr. Ebenezer Little Boyd, Francis Adams and Amariah R. Tufts. Edes, *History*, note on p. 82.

ing to the ministrations of the Rev. Dr. Morse, whose theology, even at that early date, was discredited by no small number of his parishioners." [13]

On December 28, 1815, a group of these members met and took action to establish formally the Second Congregational church of Charlestown. Many of Morse's most influential parishioners were among this group. Dr. Josiah Bartlett, his family physician, explained his reasons for withdrawing from the First church, in a lengthy letter: "I objected to . . . your constant opposition to the opinion and proceedings of the affairs of the university, to a total suspension of official interchange with the clergy at Boston and others which had formerly been maintained and to your engagement in and encouragements of controversies which I supposed injurious to yourself and to the public. . . ." He continued in detail,

The omission of interchange . . . I always considered as unfortunate and injudicious. I have esteemed them as learned, pious and exemplary men, and have often wondered why if their principles are unsound and their preaching unprofitable the usual intercourse has been, and is still maintained between them and others, whose religious sentiments are congenial to your own. . . . I repeat what I have often officially declared that I believe the Christian religion and have a firm persuasion of its truth. Though I have been greatly deficient in essential duties, I hope ever to serve its institutions and contribute to its support, but I am not yet convinced that any denomination of Christians is exclusively right, whilst all others are distinctively wrong.[14] . . .

Morse replied to Bartlett's letter claiming that "the divisions and alienations" have been caused by a "foreign influence" in the parish. "My steady aim has been to maintain, at once, christian liberality and ministerial fidelity. The war, (if I may so style it) on my part, has, in every instance, according

[13] Edes, *History of Harvard Church*, p. 82.
[14] Letter in N. Y. Public Library, Feb. 18, 1817.

to my present recollection been defensive, and, as I have believed, necessary and useful." [15]

Another loyal and faithful member of the First church also decided to withdraw quietly and join the new church. However, this man, Joseph Hurd, had such consideration for the feelings of his old "friend and pastor, the Rev. Dr. Morse . . . that he forbore to add his name to the agreement of the fifty subscribers and refrained from asking for himself and his wife a dismission from the old church to the new until the latter had been organized and entered upon its work by other hands than his." [16]

The majority who left Morse's church were of "respectability, culture and weight of influence in the town—the Russells, the Gorhams, the Austins, the Devenses, the Hurds, Bartletts, Harrises, Bradstreets, and many more being among the number." [17] However, a number of these families were split by the controversy. "Many of the old resident families had gone or were lessened in members. The Russells, for instance, were represented in name by one maiden lady, and the Gorhams by a single man (much of his life not a householder). Bradstreets, Devens, Frothingham, and others were

[15] Letter in N. Y. Public Library, Feb. 25, 1817.

[16] Edes, *History of Harvard Church*, note on pp. 123, 124. "Joseph Hurd had very few advantages of education, and this was a source of regret to him as long as he lived. But sterling good sense and activity of mind supplied the deficiency of education. As a business man he was remarkably successful, so that, while yet a young man, he withdrew from the business which he had established, and, at the age of forty, thinking that he had money enough, he was glad to free himself from the perplexities and uncertainties of trade. From that time during the remaining forty-nine years, although he afterwards entered largely into commerce, his life was one of comparative leisure, and he found time to enlarge and enrich his mind by an acquaintance with the best literary and theological works then current. Among prose writers, Franklin was, perhaps, his favorite. He seemed to know the Bible, especially the New Testament by heart, and in particular St. Paul's writings and all the texts bearing on the Unitarian controversy. He regarded as one of the most important events of his life the transferring of himself and his family from Dr. Morse's church to Mr. Prentiss'." (Henry Edes, *History of Harvard Church*, p. 264.)

[17] *Ibid.*, p. 55.

on both sides; indeed, on both sides were good and valuable people. . . . Yet it may be added that of the larger properties, most of them then newly acquired, a good deal was represented in the newer church, as also was social prominence, and a good share of the moderate number of persons in town who had a collegiate education, or that acquired by any wide study of the world." [18] The candidate for the pulpit of the new church strengthened this impression of the people in a letter to Dr. Allen: "I have been myself at Charlestown today. The society there is respectable in numbers and constantly increasing and in wealth is undoubtedly the first in town. As a proof of their ability and liberality the contribution on Thanksgiving Day, for the relief of the poor, may be cited. It amounted to $105. In Dr. Morse's society, it was $88. and in the Society of Universalists, $74." [19]

Gamaliel Bradford, who had recently come from the First church in Boston and had associated himself with Morse's church, felt inclined to join with the newly formed group. As he explained it to Morse: "A new church having been established and confirmed in this place upon principles more conformable to my faith and religious opinions, I am about to join it. . . . Not only my own inclinations, but the religious persuasions of the rest of my family inducing us to associate with it, I hope you will see this my determination of joining it with the same liberality and charitable feelings, with which you have permitted us to commune with yours." [20] Among those who remained with Morse was Jeremiah Evarts, editor of the *Panoplist* and "one of the most distinguished philanthropists at that time in the country." [21]

In spite of the controversial nature of the Charlestown pas-

[18] Hunnewell, *Sketch of Charlestown*, p. 27.
[19] Edes, *History of Harvard Church*, p. 153.
[20] Yale Letter, Charlestown, April 4, 1817.
[21] Hunnewell, *Sketch of Charlestown*, p. 41.

tor, the division in his church was conducted quietly and peacefully. Little notice of the event was taken beyond the town itself. Bentley merely remarked that the division had taken place, as if it were an inevitability. Said George E. Ellis,

I have heard from persons in this town who had means for forming an intelligent judgment in the case, that, had the pastor of the First church at the time been a man of another spirit, though holding the Orthodox creed, it is doubtful whether there would have been a secession from the church and society sufficiently strong in numbers and means to have formed a Unitarian or Liberal parish when our own was established. . . . But if Dr. Morse could not compromise, neither could he pacify nor harmonize differences. His course as a controversialist determined that action of those who formed our Society. Some of the most influential and prominent members of his church and parish initiated the movement of secession to form a Liberal Congregational church.[22]

Both parties apparently felt relieved after the separation and agreed that it was a wise move. Prentiss, the pastor of the new church, said that he was gratified with the growth of liberal principles and believed the recent controversy had positive value. . . . "From the dropping of conversation, I occasionally catch, I have no doubt that the 'cunning ones' who thought 'to ride the whirlwind and direct the storm,' sincerely wish they had never meddled with so unfortunate a business. They must feel, and I am sure they do feel, that they can no longer work the engine of terror, and that they are at last cast upon the weapons of argument, which they will wield with but little dexterity, having been so long unused to them." [23] And later he adds, "If we can give our people the religion of the understanding and the heart, that of the life will follow of necessity." [24]

[22] G. E. Ellis, *Discourse delivered in Harvard Church*, Charlestown, p. 38.
[23] Henry Edes, *History of Harvard Church*, Letter to Allen, June 24, 1817, p. 155.
[24] *Ibid.*, p. 157.

The feeling of Dr. Morse was, on the contrary, quite the opposite from that implied by the new pastor. He wrote to his aged father, "The past winter, to me, has been in many respects interesting and trying. At one time affairs in my parish wore a threatening aspect produced by Unitarian influence, which has caused a great part of my trials for the last ten years —but, through the kind interposition of Providence (often experienced before), the threatening cloud has, in a very remarkable manner dissipated and passed away. . . ." [25] In fact, Morse lost about one quarter of his church's income by the division, but within nine months he had gained eighty-three communicants, five times as many as had gone. A revival, which he interpreted as divine favor, set in upon his parish. To Dr. Lyman he communicated: "What has been by far the most interesting period of my ministry—since first October last—since that time 60 to 70 have obtained hope in this town, new cases occur daily. Some are marvelous. About 50 have or will have next Sabbath joined my church. . . . This seasonable and marvelous work has saved the church from an artful and deep-laid plan to corrupt and destroy it. But the same is broken, and we are escaped and the Lord hath done it so as to take all the glory to Himself. The adversaries have been confounded. The new society [Unitarian], which was intended to have been the instrument of our ruin, is likely to prove the instrument of our salvation. The details must be deferred till I see you. I can only say what the best men in my parish say, that though two months ago, this parish was in a deplorable state, on the verge of ruin in their view (not mine), yet now, none more promising in the State. Old prejudicies are rooted up, harmony prevails in the church. The Unitarian controversy has provided the best effects in lessening the influence of Unitarianism, both by ex-

[25] Yale Letter, March 18, 1816.

posing to the public inspection its advocates (which they have even ordained) and showing the weakness of their arguments. It has sunk 50% the influence of some of their champions." [26]

His optimism was further indicated to Bancroft Fowler of Windsor, who replied:

I rejoice to hear that, "amidst the convulsions which have shaken your town, parish and church, you have reason to think, that true religion has lost no ground among you." . . . I hope the remainder of your days will be peaceful and happy. But the faithful ministers of Christ must not calculate on permanent tranquility in this world, and especially in this age of it. For it appears to me peculiarly an age of commotions and divisions. At the same time that the friends of divine truth are laying aside their minor differences and becoming more united in promoting the cause of the Redeemer; we see, and it is what might be reasonably expected, the enemies of divine truth exciting divisions and propagating error. Satan will not suffer his kingdom to be overturned without a struggle.[27] . . .

A very short time after this letter had come to Morse, he was called upon to experience the truth of its bitter prophecy. On February 19th, he received a paper signed by twenty-five of his church members, asking him to agree with the Church in calling a Council to dissolve his pastoral relation. After the encouraging revivals, the expression of confidence by the ladies of his church (on March 27, 1817), and his optimistic attitude, this request must have come as a tremendous blow. Samuel Osgood, of the Springfield Church, who was going through a somewhat similar experience as a result of his refusal to exchange with the liberal preachers,[28] wrote to Morse:

I sincerely sympathize with you and with every faithful minister of Christ who is exposed to the persecuting rage of Unitarian liberality.

[26] Yale Letter, March 4, 1817.
[27] Yale Letter, Jan. 19, 1819.
[28] See W. B. Sprague, *Discourse at Funeral of Samuel Osgood*, 1863, p. 25.

. . . I trust you will not be induced to give up so important a post because of a little hard fighting. God is our shield and he will protect us from all our adversaries. I hope, dear sir, that we may pray for one another and hold fast our profession without wavering. These are trying times, but let us remember that they that are approved shall be made manifest. May we and all the faithful servants of our Lord stand in one lot and be accepted of him in the day of his appearing.[29]

However, his family and his friends in the neighborhood advised him to withdraw quietly from the scene which had been his battlefield for so many years. His failing health encouraged him to consent but his strong and unflinching sense of duty made him reluctant to give up. The Hopkinsians of Andover addressed a letter to him, "expressing deep regret in view of the loss of his influence to various important objects, necessarily consequent upon his removal from that region, and yet, from a regard to his own personal comfort, advising on the whole, to the resignation of his pastoral charge." [30]

Morse had already relinquished the leadership of the orthodox to his Hopkinsian friends and no doubt felt that his work was done. Consequently, on Sunday, August 29th, 1819, he announced to his congregation his intention to resign. It was the last time he was ever to appear before the Charlestown church as their pastor. His attitude is reflected in his remarks:

For more than thirty years past, in a very peculiar and convulsed state of the world, amidst the rise and rapid propagation among us of insidious and dangerous errors, which have assailed us on every side, and which I have felt it my duty to expose and resist, I have endeavored faithfully, and though in much imperfection, to watch over you, to guard you and to feed you with the bread of life, and to take care of the lambs of my flock. . . . As regards myself, I view the dissolution of my pastoral relation to you as a release from a station of great responsibility, of arduous and constant warfare; as a relief from cares

[29] Yale Letter, March 30, 1819.
[30] W. B. Sprague, *Life of Jedidiah Morse*, p. 42.

long sustained, which have impaired my health, and have become a burden too weighty for my years and my slender constitution. . . . In what manner this event is to affect the interests of this Church and Parish, and the cause of religion in this region, cannot be foreseen.[31]

Thus closed the controversial career of the Charlestown divine. He "left this neighborhood in the height of the angry strife which he had inflamed," says Ellis. "He had a right to assume the championship of a cause which he professed was dearer to him than life. Men certainly his superiors in all virtues and saintliness had maintained the divine authority and the loneliness of Calvinism. We may allow much to his natural sorrow and the disturbance of the equipose of his temper as he saw his old historic church and parish, where Harvard and Shepherd and Morton had ministered, wasting away, because the irresistible developments of human progress around him had brought his Calvinistic creed into discredit, not to say into undisguised contempt, among those whom he met in his daily walks." [32]

The battle-scarred and weary warrior of orthodoxy sought exile among the Indians gathering facts and laying plans "for the rescue of these outcasts." [33]

---

[31] *Ibid.*, p. 43.

[32] G. E. Ellis, *Discourse*, p. 36.

[33] W. B. Sprague, *Life of Jedidiah Morse*, p. 172. Morse was appointed by the President of the United States and Congress to investigate and report on the condition of the Indian tribes of the country. In 1822 he included an introductory letter in the published report stating that if it shall "prove instrumental in awakening the attention of others to the state of these neglected and oppressed people and of laying foundations for future civil, social and religious improvement and happiness, he would have no regret." He submitted it to those engaged in imparting "the blessings of civilization and Christianity to these untutored, heathen tribes and to the people generally in this favored country." (Jedidiah Morse, *A Report to the Secretary of War of the United States, on Indian Affairs* . . . New Haven, 1822, pp. 9, 10.)

BIBLIOGRAPHY

A LIST OF SELECTED, UNPUBLISHED LETTERS

YALE UNIVERSITY LIBRARY: A COLLECTION
OF "THE FAMILY PAPERS OF JEDIDIAH MORSE, D.D."

Cited in the
following pages
of this book

Nov. 28, 1779: Letter from Jedidiah Morse to his parents. 19, 20

Feb. 20, 1781: Letter from Jedidiah Morse to his parents. 20, 21

Jan. 6, 1782: Letter from Morse to his parents. 19, 22

April 11, 1784: Letter from Morse at New Haven, to his parents.   25

March 29, 1785: Letter from Morse to his father stating his hope of a Christian life—"truly benevolent, even Christian temper and disposition." . . . .

Nov. 15, 1788: Letter from Dr. Rogers of Philadelphia to Dr. Belknap. [Part published in *Belknap Papers*.]   29

Feb. 27, 1792: Letter from Henry Channing to J. Morse on conformity to the times and on the treatment of Universalists. . . . .

April 8, 1795: Letter from Channing to J. Morse on church government. . . . .

Nov. 12, 1796: Letter from Channing to J. Morse on church government. . . . .

March 7, 1796: Letter from John Erskine of Edinburgh to J. Morse, speaking of the Divinity of Christ. . . . .

March 12, 1799: Letter from William Wells of Brattle-

BIBLIOGRAPHY

BIBLIOGRAPHY

Cited in the following pages of this book

July 19, 1815: Letter from J. Morse to his son, Samuel
  Finley Breese. 147, 148
Dec. 12, 1815: Letter from J. Morse to Luther Rice of
  Kentucky. 142
March 18, 1816: Letter from J. Morse to his father. .. 158
March 4, 1817: Letter from Morse to Lyman. 158, 159
April 4, 1817: Letter from G. Bradford to J. Morse. 156
November 24, 1817: Letter from Luther Rice to J.
  Morse. 142, 143
Jan. 19, 1819: Letter from B. Fowler to J. Morse. 159
March 30, 1819: Letter from Samuel Osgood to
  J. Morse. 159, 160

NEW YORK CITY PUBLIC LIBRARY: COLLECTION
OF JEDIDIAH MORSE LETTERS

March 1, 1815: Letter from Enoch Hale to J. Morse. 143
March 17, 1815: Letter from Dr. J. Lyman to J.
  Morse. 143, 144
March 27, 1815: Letter from Dr. J. Lathrop to J.
  Morse. 144
April 12, 1815: Letter from Ashbel Green to J. Morse. 152
Sept. 9, 1815: Letter from W. Wilberforce to J. Morse. 137
Dec. 13, 1815: Letter from Jeremiah Evarts to Rev.
  Luther Rice. 142
Feb. 18, 1817: Letter from Dr. Josiah Bartlett to
  Jedidiah Morse. 154
Feb. 25, 1817: Letter from J. Morse to Dr. Bartlett. 154, 155

ESSEX INSTITUTE, SALEM, MASSACHUSETTS.

VOL. I. NOS. 55, 56

1797: Letter from F. Nichols of Boston to William
  Bentley. 41
Jan. 28, 1799: Letter from F. Nichols to William
  Bentley. 56, 57

BIBLIOGRAPHY

*Cited in the
following pages
of this book*

CONNECTICUT HISTORICAL SOCIETY
April 15, 1799: Published letter circularized among the
ministers of the state.   62

PERIODICALS AND NEWSPAPERS

Boston Daily Advertiser, November 9, 1882.
Boston Patriot, May 13, 1815.
Boston Recorder.
Columbian Centinel (Boston). Copies in New York Public Library.
Congregational Quarterly, Vol. I, No. 2, April, 1859 (Boston).
Congregationalist, November 27, 1857 (Boston).
General Repository and Review, Vol. II, 1813 (Cambridge, Mass.).
Historical Magazine, New Series, Vol. IX, No. IV and V, April and
May, 1871 (Boston and New York).
Journal of American Educational Society, February, 1838 (Boston).
Massachusetts Missionary Magazine, Vols. I–III (Boston, 1803–5).
Monthly Anthology (Boston).
Monthly Religious Magazine, Vol. 31, February, 1864 (Boston).
Panoplist, Vols. I–VI, VIII (Boston).
Spirit of the Pilgrims, Vol. II (Boston, 1829).

MEMOIRS, DIARIES, SERMONS, ETC.

Andover, Memorial of the Semi-Centennial Celebration of Founding
of Theological Seminary at Andover (Andover, 1859).
Alexander, James, Life of Archibald Alexander (New York, 1854).
Allen, William, Memoir of John Codman, with Reminiscences by
Joshua Bates (Boston, 1853).
Bacon, Leonard, Commemorative Discourse on Andover Theological
Seminary (Andover, 1858).
——, Historical Discourse in the First Church, New Haven, Con-
necticut, with an appendix (New Haven and New York, 1839).

BIBLIOGRAPHY

Beecher, Lyman, Autobiography and Correspondence of Lyman Beecher, edited by Charles Beecher (New York, 1864, 1865).

Belknap, Jeremy, Life of Jeremy Belknap, collected and arranged by his granddaughter (New York, 1847).

Belknap, Jeremy, Sermon preached at the Installation of Rev. Jedidiah Morse, Charlestown, Massachusetts, April 30, 1789 (Boston, 1789).

Bentley, William, Diary of William Bentley, Vols. I–IV. (Essex Institute, Salem, Mass., 1905–14).

——, Sermon preached at the Stone Chapel, Boston, September 12, 1790 (Boston, 1790).

Dwight, Timothy, Sermon on the Nature and Danger of Infidel Philosophy, September 9, 1797 (New Haven, 1797).

Edwards, Tryon, The Works of Rev. Joseph Bellamy, with a Memoir of His Life and Character (Boston, 1850).

Ellis, George E., Discourse on the 25th Anniversary of His Ordination, March 12, 1865, Harvard Church, Charlestown, Mass.

Emmons, Nathanael, Sermon preached before Convention of Congregational Ministers in Boston, May 31, 1804 (Boston, 1804).

Fisher, George P., Discourse Commemorative of the History of the Church of Christ in Yale College (New Haven, 1858).

Gannett, William Channing, Memoir of Ezra Stiles Gannett (Boston, 1875).

Groce, George C., Jr., Benjamin Gale (New England Quarterly, Vol. X, No. 4, 1937).

Holmes, Abiel, The Life of Ezra Stiles (Boston, 1798).

Jones, Joseph H., The Life of Ashbel Green (New York, 1849).

Lawrence, Edward A., Discourse at the Funeral of Leonard Woods, August 28, 1854 (Boston, 1854).

Lee, Eliza Buckminster, Memoir of the Rev. Joseph Buckminster, D. D., and of His Son Rev. Joseph S. Buckminster (Boston, 1851).

Miller, Robert C., Historical Discourse on the 50th Anniversary of the First Baptist Church of Salem, Massachusetts.

Morse, Jedidiah, Sermon on National Fast, May 9, 1798 (Boston, 1798).

——, Sermon Preached at Charlestown, Mass., on November 29, 1798, on the Anniversary of Thanksgiving (Boston, 1799).

——, Sermon Exhibiting the Present Dangers and Consequent

BIBLIOGRAPHY

Duties of the Citizens of the United States of America, April 25, 1799 (New York, 1799).

———, Sermon at Boston at the Ordination of the Rev. Joshua Huntington (Boston, 1808).

———, Sermon Delivered before the Convention of Congregational Ministers in Boston, May 28, 1812 (Boston, 1812).

Park, Edward A., Memoir of Nathanael Emmons (Boston, 1861).

Prime, S. I., Life of Samuel F. B. Morse (New York, 1875).

Sprague, William B., Annals of the American Pulpit, Vols. I and II (New York, 1857).

———, Discourse at the Funeral of Samuel Osgood, Dec. 12, 1862, in Springfield, Mass. (Albany, 1863).

———, Life of Jedidiah Morse (New York, 1874).

Spring, Gardiner, Personal Reminiscences of the Life and Times of Gardiner Spring, Vol. I (New York, 1866).

Stiles, Ezra, The Literary Diary of Ezra Stiles, edited by Franklin Bowditch Dexter (New York, 1901).

Tracy, Ebenezer Carter, Memoir of the Life of Jeremiah Evarts (Boston, 1845).

Ware, William, American Unitarian Biography, Vol. I (Boston and Cambridge, 1850).

Wells, William, Some Observations Taken in Part from an Address in Brattleborough on July 7, 1816 (Brattleboro, 1816).

Willard, Samuel, Historical Sermon at Deerfield, September 22, 1858 (Greenfield, Mass., 1858).

Willard, Sidney, Memoir of Youth and Manhood, Vols. I and II (Cambridge, 1855).

Worcester, S. M., Life and Labors of Rev. Samuel Worcester, Vol. I and II (Boston, 1852).

GENERAL REFERENCES

Andover, Collection of Documents of Andover Theological Seminary.

Allen, Joseph Henry, and Richard Eddy, History of the Unitarians and Universalists in the United States, "American Church History Series," Vol. X (New York, 1894).

Baldwin, Alice Mary, The New England Clergy and the American Revolution (Durham, North Carolina, 1928).

Baldwin, Ebenezer, History of Yale College (New Haven, 1841).

Belknap Papers in the Massachusetts Historical Society Collection, Vol. III, 5th Series, Part 2, and Vol. IV, 6th Series.

Bowen, Clarence Winthrop, Woodstock: an Historical Sketch (New York and London, 1886).

———, History of Woodstock, Connecticut (Plimpton Press, Norwood, Mass., 1926).

Budington, William I., History of the First Church, Charlestown, Massachusetts (Boston, 1845).

Calder, Isabel MacBeath, Letters and Papers of Ezra Stiles (New York, 1933).

Chadwick, John White, William Ellery Channing, Minister of Religion (Boston and New York, 1903).

Charlestown, Massachusetts, Church Papers (in Congregational Library, Boston).

Clark, Joseph S., Historical Sketch of the Congregational Churches in Massachusetts, 1620–1858 (Boston, 1858).

Dorchester, Massachusetts, Memorial of the Proprietors of the New South Meeting House in Dorchester (Boston, 1813).

———, Proceedings of the Second Church and Parish in Dorchester, Massachusetts (Boston, 1812).

Edes, Henry, History of the Harvard Church in Charlestown, Massachusetts, 1815–1879 (Boston, 1879).

Ellis, George E., The Associate Creed of Andover Theological Seminary (Boston, 1883).

———, A Half-Century of the Unitarian Controversy (London, 1858).

Ely, Ezra Stiles, A Contrast between Calvinism and Hopkinsianism (New York, 1811).

Evarts, Jeremiah, Review of American Unitarianism, Extracted from the *Panoplist*, June, 1815.

———, Review of Dorchester Controversy, from the *Panoplist*, 1814.

Fisher, George P., Discussions in History and Theology (New York, 1880).

Foster, Frank Hugh, A Genetic History of the New England Theology (Chicago, 1907).

Gambrell, Mary Latimer, Ministerial Training in 18th Century New England (New York, 1937).

Goodrich, Professor Elizur, Revivals of Religion in Yale College Journal of American Educational Society (Boston, 1838).

Greene, Evarts Boutell, The Foundation of American Nationality (New York, 1935).

Haroutunian, Joseph, Piety versus Moralism; the Passing of the New England Theology (New York, 1932).

Hill, Hamilton Andrews, History of the Old South Church, Vol. II (Boston and New York, 1890).

Hill, William, History of the Rise, Progress . . . of American Presbyterianism (Washington City, 1839).

Howe, M. A. DeWolfe, Journal of Proceedings of the Society Which Conducts the Monthly Anthology and Boston Review (Columbia Press, 1910).

Humphrey, Edward Frank, Nationalism and Religion in America, 1774–1789 (Boston, 1924).

Hunnewell, James F., Historical Sketch of Charlestown, Massachusetts.

———, A Century of Town Life: History of Charlestown, Mass., 1775 1887 (Boston, 1888).

Koch, Gustaf Adolf, Republican Religion (New York, 1933).

Larned, Ellen D., Historical Gleanings in Windham County (Providence, R. I., 1899).

———, History of Windham County, Connecticut (Worcester, Mass., 1880).

Lowell, John, Are You a Christian or a Calvinist? Published anonymously (Boston, 1815).

Morison, Samuel Eliot, Three Centuries of Harvard, 1636–1936 (Cambridge, Mass., 1936).

Morais, Herbert M., Deism in Eighteenth Century America (New York, 1934).

Morse, Jedidiah, An Appeal to the Public on the Controversy Respecting the Revolution in Harvard College . . . Charlestown, Massachusetts (Charlestown, Mass., 1814).

———, An Inquiry into the Right to Change the Ecclesiastical Constitution of the Congregational Churches of Massachusetts . . . to Which Is Prefixed Dr. Morse's Report to the General Association of Massachusetts from the *Panoplist* of August, 1815 (Boston, 1816).

———, Report to the Secretary of War of the United States on Indian Affairs (New Haven, 1822).

———, Review of American Unitarianism; or, A Brief History of the Progress and Present State of the Unitarian Churches in America . . . without Note or Alteration Extracted from the *Panoplist* (Boston, 1815).

———, True Reasons on Which the Election of a Hollis Professor . . . Was Opposed at Harvard . . . (Charlestown, Mass., 1805).

Memorial of the Semi-Centennial Celebration of the Founding of the Theological Seminary at Andover (Andover, 1859).

Old South Leaflets, Vol. VI (Boston, 1896–19—).

Park, Edward A., The Associated Creed of Andover Theological Seminary (Boston, 1883).

Quincy, Josiah, The History of Harvard University, Vols. I and II (Boston, 1840).

Reynolds, J. B., S. H. Fisher, and H. B. Wright, Two Centuries of Christian Activity at Yale (New York and London, 1901).

Riley, Isaac W., American Thought from Puritanism to Pragmatism (New York, 1915).

Rowe, Henry K., History of Andover Theological Seminary (Newton, Mass., 1933).

Stauffer, Vernon, New England and the Bavarian Illuminati (New York, 1918).

Sweet, William Warren, The Story of Religions in America (New York and London, 1930).

Thornton, John Wingate, The Pulpit of the American Revolution (Boston, 1876).

Trumbull, Benjamin, A Complete History of Connecticut, Vol. I (Hartford, 1797).

Walker, Williston, Ten New England Leaders (New York and Boston, 1901).

Wilson, James, Letters to the Rev. Ezra Stiles Ely, A.M., Author of a Contrast between Calvinism and Hopkinsianism (Boston, 1814).

Winsor, Justin, The Memorial History of Boston (Boston, 1880, 1881).

Withington, L., Contributions to the Ecclesiastical History of Essex County, Mass. (Boston, 1865).

Woods, Leonard, History of Andover Theological Seminary (Boston, 1885).

INDEX

Abbot, Samuel: bequest to Phillips Academy, 105; suspicious of Hopkinsian influence, 113

Adams, Hannah, 99-100, 143, 146

Adams, John, 32, 147

Alden, Timothy, 102

Alexander, Archibald, 83, 84

American Geography: fame of, admits Morse to cultured groups, 42; criticized, 45, 98

American Unitarianism (Morse), 145n

Anabaptists, 40

Andover Theological Seminary: founding of, 101-20; united Calvinistic support sought, 104-15; broad constitution of, 106; Calvinists yield to Hopkinsians over, 114-16; dominated by Hopkinsians, 141; Hopkinsians at, advise Morse's retirement, 160

"Appeal to the Public . . . An," 100

Appleton, Jesse, candidate for Hollis professorship, 88-89

"Are you a Christian or a Calvinist?" (Lowell), vii, 148

Arians: prevalence in Boston, 36, 47; Ware classed with, 92, 94

Arminians, 5, 66, 74; prevalence in Boston, 36, 47, 70; fear of influence of, at Harvard, 87; Ware classed with, 92, 94; excluded from Calvinists, 98, 143

Association, General, *see* General Association

Associations: efforts to coöperate with Presbyterians, 59-62; to promote coöperation among Massachusetts orthodox, 62-74; need of meetings, 64; divided opinions of, on coöperation, 67-71

Austin, Samuel, 27, 28, 107; editor *Massachusetts Missionary Magazine,* 80

Baptists, 63

Bartlet, William: contributor to theological seminary, 103, 107; urges Griffin for Andover post, 126-29; relation to new church, 126, 128, 129

Bartlett, Josiah, quoted, 154

Bates, Joshua, 102, 138

Beecher, Lyman, 51

Belknap, Jeremy, 35, 36; factor in Morse's settlement, 29-34; quoted, 31, 41

Bellamy, Joseph, 5, 9

Belsham, Thomas, 92; *Memoirs of the Life of Theophilus Lindsey,* 144; Morse publishes review of book, 145-47

Bentley, William: quoted, 36, 39, 70, 86, 96, 115; representative of liberalized religion, 38; comments of, 45, 47, 80, 99, 101, 118, 131, 139, 144, 157; religious attitude, 93

"Beware of Counterfeits" (Morse), 46

Boston: religious atmosphere of, 35-38; commercial and intellectual center, 37; cultured groups open to Morse, 42

Boston Association: welcomes Morse, 35; diverse theological sentiments of, 36, 59; opposes Hopkinsianism, 139

Bradbury, Jemima, 17

Bradford, Alden, 39

173